Something Old,
SOMETHING NEW

Hymns to Explore
Things to Do

General Themes—Who Is Jesus?

Beverly S. Bailey
John D. Horman
Suzi Gifford

Edited by Mary Nelson Keithahn

Abingdon Press
Nashville

00 01 02 03 04 05 06 07 08 09 — 10 9 8 7 6 5 4 3 2 1

MANUFACTURED IN THE UNITED STATES OF AMERICA

Contents

Preface

A New Approach to Children's Ministry

After many years of involvement in children's ministry as a church educator, curriculum writer, choir director, and pastor, I have learned that churches need to take a more holistic approach to working with children, especially in an age when we have less and less of their time. A church school class should sing hymns that not only relate to the biblical and historical content of the curriculum, but that will also be encountered in congregational worship. A children's choir should know something about the biblical and historical background of the hymns and anthems they sing. Congregational worship should be planned to allow children to participate in singing, reading, and proclaiming the Word with understanding and enthusiasm. In every church setting where children are involved, they should be given opportunities to expand their vocabulary of faith, develop skills in worship, respond to God's Word in creative ways, and experience the joy of sharing their gifts with the congregation.

The Best of Holistic Ministry with Children

This course began with the dream of a church musician, a church educator, and an artist. Using classic and contemporary hymns, biblical stories and other scripture, and unusual creative art media, they designed learning experiences for children, youth, and multigenerational groups around important concepts of the Christian faith. After testing their approach for several years in a variety of settings, they have developed this course to share with others.

The learning activities suggested for each session are all age-appropriate, related to the session objectives, and organized in logical lesson plans. As the children listen to stories and other readings from the Bible, they will also learn something about the background of each scripture, discover the meaning of unfamiliar terms, and consider the relevance of the scripture for today. In addition to getting acquainted with the texts and tunes of twelve hymns, the children will gain experience in sightsinging, ear training, imitating rhythm patterns, singing expressively, choreographing a hymn, and playing in a percussion ensemble. The art projects will introduce them to new media of expression, and allow them to respond to the Bible stories and hymns in creative ways. Individual take-home projects will provide opportunities for the children to share with their families what they have been learning at church. Their group projects, saved for use in the last session or given to others, will enable them to share their experiences with the larger faith community.

A Valuable Course for Teachers

In each session, there is background material for the teacher on the scripture and the text and tune of the hymn. The clearly stated purpose and objectives provide useful guidelines for planning. The teaching techniques and learning activities suggested are easy to follow and can serve as models for teachers to use in other settings.

A Learning Experience for the Whole Church

It has been my experience that whenever a church takes a holistic approach to children's ministry, the whole congregation benefits. What the children learn in this course will not only help them become an integral part of the church now, but will also prepare them for their roles as persons of faith in the church of the future.

Mary Nelson Keithahn

About This Course

The Purpose

This course is designed to help children discover more about who Jesus was, what he meant to his followers, and how he still helps us today. The learning activities are planned around hymns, Bible study, and creative art.

There are two sessions each on Jesus' roles as Shepherd, Advocate, Way to God, Leader, Finest Friend, and Teacher. One of these paired sessions introduces the children to a classic, familiar hymn, and the other to a newly composed, contemporary hymn.* The final session is a hymn sing that provides an opportunity for the children to review what they have learned and share it with their families and/or members of the congregation. All the hymns used are included in this book, and may be reproduced in quantities as needed for the course.

How the Course Can Be Used

These thirteen sessions may be used as an alternative curriculum for a church school quarter or as part of a midweek integrated program of education, music, and worship for children and/or multi-generational groups.

The course may also be used in vacation Bible school settings by selecting one of the paired lesson plans for each extended two-hour session.

In addition, since each session is self-contained, any one of them may be used by itself for a special event (e.g., a program for children accompanying their parents to an all-church retreat) in conjunction with other curriculum content on a related theme, or in a choir day camp or retreat.

Leadership Possibilities

This course is designed so that a variety of gifted persons can play an important role in the life of children. When considering the leadership for each session, look at a variety of teaching models for the sessions. These sessions are particularly exciting for the leadership and the children alike when a team of persons shares responsibilities in ways that match their gifts and talents. Look for persons who truly enjoy working with children. If you have someone who can play the piano but does not feel comfortable leading the music portions of the sessions, team them with another person who may not have piano skills. Perhaps one of the children is able to play piano to assist in some of the music games. Consider asking a guest musician to come and lead the music in some of the sessions. Ask someone to make a tape recording of all the hymns so that you have them to play for the children. Perhaps one person would be willing to collect and prepare the art supplies and another would be willing to meet in the session with the children to lead them through the process of creating their artwork. There may be someone in your setting who is gifted in drama. Ask him or her to come and lead the children in the sessions that involve drama.

This series is designed to be used in a wide variety of settings and leadership styles. Consider this an opportunity to be creative and flexible in choosing leadership.

Resources Needed
- Bible
- Piano or keyboard
- Chalkboard or chart board
- Black and colored markers
- Art supplies, most of which are available at arts and crafts stores

It would be wise to look at the materials needed for each session as you begin the course, in case you need to order supplies.

Hymn Sing in Session Seven

The scripted order of worship for the hymn sing in Session Seven uses all twelve hymns from this course and involves the children in leadership roles. This hymn sing could be planned as the last session of this course with parents invited to attend; as a special event in conjunction with a Sunday or midweek multigenerational supper; or as an alternative to traditional Sunday morning worship.

If you want to involve the congregation in the hymn sing, be sure to meet early in the course with your pastors, organist, and worship committee to plan the event and schedule the date. Emphasize that this event will be more than a joyous end-of-course celebration. It will also help the children discover how the hymns they have learned can be used in a worship order and provide opportunities for them to experience leading worship. The hymn sing will also give pastors a chance to work with children in a new way.

You may also want to ask these worship planners whether some or all of the hymns from this course could be sung in your Sunday worship during this quarter. This would be meaningful to children who attend worship with their families, and would also help to prepare the congregation to participate in the hymn sing.

If you plan to share the hymn sing with the whole congregation outside of class time, use Session Seven to help the children prepare for the service.

* Selected from Mary Nelson Keithahn and John D. Horman, *Come Away with Me: A Collection of Original Hymns* (Nashville: Abingdon Press, 1998); and Keithahn and Horman, *Time Now to Gather: New Hymns for the Church Family* (Nashville: Abingdon Press, 1998).

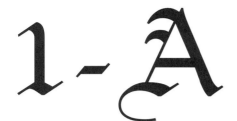

Who Is Jesus?
Our Shepherd

Something Old: "The King of Love My Shepherd Is"

Purpose: To introduce children to the biblical concept of a *shepherd* and help them discover how to be shepherds today.

Objectives: After participating in this session, children may be able to:
1. Describe the role of a shepherd in biblical times.
2. Tell why we call God "Shepherd."
3. Identify "The King of Love My Shepherd Is" by its tune, and sing one stanza.
4. Show how people act as shepherds today.

Materials Needed
- Bibles
- Copies of the shepherd picture and the hymn for each child (pages 13 and 66)
- Piano or keyboard
- Orff-type instruments: alto and bass xylophones, glockenspiel, and metallophone (optional)
- Display board or chart board
- Markers
- Shepherd costumes for each child: Fabric headpieces; optional robes or drapes with belts; shepherd props (a staff or crook, pouch, sling, horn of oil, wooden flute, lamb puppet or stuffed toy lamb)
- Art supplies: Felt in several skin-color tones (enough for a six-inch square for each child); eight-inch-square felt pieces in bright colors (one per child); additional felt in contrasting colors; brightly colored knitting yarn cut in six-inch strands (three for each banner); a nine-inch-long dowel for each child; white glue; scissors; plastic eyes or small black buttons (one per child)
- Camera (optional)

Background for the Leader

Scripture: Isaiah 40:11; Ezekiel 34:12; Psalm 23; John 10:11-14

The work of a shepherd is detailed in the first two passages. Isaiah 40:11 describes the nurturing qualities of the one who is to come (the *Messiah* or "anointed one"). It is one of the texts included in Handel's *Messiah*. Ezekiel 34:12 describes a shepherd as one who searches out and rescues the sheep who have been scattered.

Psalm 23 compares God's relationship to us with that of a shepherd to the flock. It is a comforting song, reassuring us that we are in God's care. The children may already be familiar with this psalm.

John 10:11-14 contains one of the famous "I am" statements that Jesus used to explain who he was and what God had called him to do. Jesus is the good and faithful shepherd who will sacrifice himself for the sake of the flock.

Hymn: "The King of Love My Shepherd Is" (ST. COLUMBA)

Text: "The King of Love My Shepherd Is" is a metrical paraphrase of Psalm 23 that was written by Henry Baker in 1868. Baker was not content with rewriting the psalm so it could be sung to a tune in simple meter like a hymn. He made the psalm a Christian hymn by adding New Testament references to the nature and role of Jesus in every stanza: living water and celestial food, King of love and Good Shepherd, unction (healing) grace, cross and chalice. Many of these concepts come from the Gospel of John. The children will grow into these ideas later. For now, focus on the concept of Jesus as the Good Shepherd. This is one of the earliest metaphors Christians used to understand the role of Jesus in their lives. A picture of a shepherd carrying a lamb on his shoulders (stanza 3) was found in the catacombs of Rome.

Tune: ST. COLUMBA is an Irish melody named for the man who brought Christianity to Scotland. It was first published in 1855 in Dr. George Petrie's collection of old Irish airs.

Preparation

- Reproduce the hymn and shepherd pages for each child.
- Gather the shepherd costumes and props.
- Mark Bibles with the scripture references the children will read.
- Enlarge the acrostic on the display board or a chart (see page 12).
- Practice the hymn.
- Assemble the art supplies.
- Prepare the banner as follows: For each child, cut a six-inch square from skin-colored felt, an eight-inch square from brightly colored felt, and three 1" x 3" tabs from felt in contrasting colors. Fold three felt tabs over the top edge of each eight-inch square, allowing each tab to overlap one inch on the front and back of the square (see page 11). Thread one six-inch strand of colored yarn through each tab with a needle and tie in a bow. This will serve as the casing for the dowel.
- Optional: Copy page 89 for a take-home coloring page (one per child).

The Session

1. Playing a Singing Game. As the children gather, use this pitch-matching game to encourage individual and group singing and introduce the concept of a *shepherd*. Latecomers can easily be incorporated into this activity as they arrive.

Teach the song by singing one phrase at a time for the children to echo. When they are comfortable with it, have the children close their eyes. Ask those who would like to be the "lost sheep" to raise their hands. Choose one child to hide anywhere in the room while the others keep their eyes closed. Sing the song again, with the "lost sheep" singing the echo

The Lost Sheep

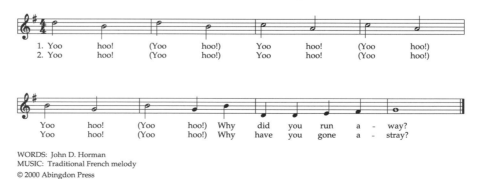

1. Yoo hoo! (Yoo hoo!) Yoo hoo! (Yoo hoo!)
2. Yoo hoo! (Yoo hoo!) Yoo hoo! (Yoo hoo!)

Yoo hoo! (Yoo hoo!) Why did you run a - way?
Yoo hoo! (Yoo hoo!) Why have you gone a - stray?

WORDS: John D. Horman
MUSIC: Traditional French melody
© 2000 Abingdon Press

alone, until the other children guess his or her identity and hiding place. Repeat as often as time allows, letting the children take turns being the "lost sheep." (*Seven to eight minutes*)

2. Exploring the Role of Shepherds. This activity explores the role of shepherds through Bible study, a picture, and dramatic play. Have the children sit where they can see you and one another. Ask: "What is a shepherd? What do shepherds do?" After the children have shared their ideas, suggest that they see what the Bible says about shepherds. Choose older children to read the four scripture references you have marked in the Bibles: Isaiah 40:11; Ezekiel 34:12; Psalm 23; and John 10:11-14. After each passage is read, record what it says about shepherds on the display board or a chart. (If you plan to use Session 1-B, save this list to help the children recall what they learn about shepherds in this session.)

Give each child a copy of the shepherd page and have them look at the illustration (see page 13). Discuss together what shepherds wear and what they carry with them and why. When you have finished, gather up the papers to use later in the session.

Have ready a variety of clothing shepherds might wear so the children can dress up and pretend they are caring for the sheep. If biblical costumes for children are not available, improvise headpieces from 18" x 24" pieces of fabric with roping for ties. Drape larger pieces of fabric around the children for robes and belt in place. Let them choose a prop to carry. After all the children are in costume, ask them to look at their hands and think about how shepherds use their hands in their work. Suggest that they act out their ideas. For example, a child might rescue a lamb from a thicket, pour oil on a lamb's wound, carry a lost lamb home, build a stone fence to protect the flock, guide the sheep to a new pasture. Before the children take off their costumes, take some pictures of them to display later. (*Fifteen to eighteen minutes*)

3. Learning the Hymn. The tune ST. COLUMBA is simple to teach because it has a range of only one octave. Assign a number to each note of the scale, using the numbers 1-8, with "1" as the lowest pitch and "8" as the highest.

You may want to enlarge this scale on the display board or chart so you can point to the numbers as you sing.

Pass out copies of the hymn to the children. Before you ask them to sing the words, sing the tune with the numbers, line by line, for them to echo. This will help them sense the relationship between pitches.

Next, sing the first stanza of the hymn, beginning with the first line and adding one line at a time until they have echoed the whole stanza. If there is time, and instruments are available, you may want to add the Orff-style accompaniment printed on page 67.

The language used in this hymn includes words that are not commonly spoken today. You may want to read the corresponding verses from Psalm 23 after each stanza is sung to help the children see the relationship between the two songs. You may also want to mention the use of the Good Shepherd symbol for Jesus in the catacombs. (*Ten to twelve minutes*)

4. Making Individual "Sheep" Banners. Introduce the project by asking the children to think about all the ways shepherds use their hands in caring for the sheep. Let each child

choose one of the six-inch squares. Have them lay one hand on the square, with fingers spread out as widely as possible (especially the thumb). Trace around their hands with a pencil, and carefully cut the shapes from the felt. Pass out the banners you prepared before the session, and show the children how to glue the hand onto the felt in an upside-down position (see page 11) so that it looks like a sheep. Give each one a handful of batting to glue to the "sheep," leaving half of the fingers and the thumb uncovered, and an "eye" to glue on the thumb. When the glue is dry, slip a dowel through the tabs of each banner. Let the children take their banners home or display them in the classroom. *(Fifteen minutes)*

5. Sharing a Puzzle and a Prayer. Gather the children around the display board or chart where you have printed this acrostic:

```
        S __ __ __ __
   __ H __ __ __
   __ E __
        P __ __ __ __
        H __ __ __
   __ E __ __ __
__ __ R __
__ __ D
```

(Words to use: stray, harm, fed, psalm, sheep, Jesus, care, God)

Pass out the shepherd page again, and have the children look at the prayer:

God, you care for us like a shepherd.
You see that we are fed,
find us when we stray,
and keep us from all harm.
We are like sheep,
and sometimes lose our way,
but you sent Jesus, our Good Shepherd,
to bring us home to you.
For this, we sing our psalm of praise.
Be with us now, and all our days.
Amen.

Explain that they can find words for the acrostic in the prayer. List the words on the board or chart as they are named, and then have the children help decide where they fit into the puzzle. (If your group includes younger children, read the prayer aloud so they can hear the words and participate in the process.) When the puzzle is completed, read the prayer aloud together. *(Eight to ten minutes)*

Questions for Reflection————————

- What did you see and hear that showed what the children learned about the role of shepherds in Bible times?
- How did the hymn help the children connect the concepts of God as our Shepherd and Jesus as the Good Shepherd?
- How has this session helped the children think about ways they may be shepherds today?

God, you care for us like a shepherd.
You see that we are fed,
find us when we stray,
and keep us from all harm.
We are like sheep,
and sometimes lose our way,
but you sent Jesus, our Good Shepherd,
to bring us home to you.
For this, we sing our psalm of praise.
Be with us now, and all our days.
Amen.

Shepherds wore a cloth headcover for protection from sun and dust, a woolen tunic covered by a mantle, which was also used as a warm blanket, a belt to hold their valuables, and sandals on their feet. They carried a staff to help guide the sheep and for climbing. Shepherds also carried a rod or heavy stick, a pouch to carry food, tools, and stones for their leather sling.

1-B Who Is Jesus? Our Shepherd

Something New: "There Is a Need for Shepherds"

Purpose: To introduce children to the biblical concept of a *shepherd*, and to help them discover how to be shepherds today.

Objectives: After participating in this session, children may be able to:
1. Sing a new hymn, "There Is a Need for Shepherds."
2. Identify some of the shepherds at work in today's world.
3. Construct a "Shepherds Today" banner to give to a community service organization.

Materials Needed

- Bibles
- Copies of the hymn for each child (page 68)
- Piano or keyboard
- Display board or chart board
- Markers
- List of what a shepherd does from Session 1-A
- Shepherd Riddle Cards (page 17)
- Hats and/or props to suggest the occupations illustrated on the cards
- Materials for the banner: A piece of 3" x 5" fabric backing in a bright color (use burlap, woven upholstery or drapery fabric, or double knit); one 1/4-inch dowel, thirty-six inches long; cord for hanging banner; six-inch squares of felt in varying skin tones, one per child; two- to three-inch-high precut letters in brightly colored felt for words on the banner; darning needle; felt scraps in all colors; scissors; white fabric glue; brightly colored yarn cut in eight-inch strands; tubes of puffy and glitter fabric paints in bright colors

Background for the Leader

Scripture: Ezekiel 34:15-16; John 21:15-17

Both passages stress that shepherds must be responsible caregivers. Ezekiel 34:15-16 is a continuation of the passage used in Session 1-A. It identifies God as the shepherd of the flock, and outlines the shepherd's role: to seek the lost, bring back the strayed, bind up the injured, strengthen the weak, and see that there is justice for all.

John 21:15-17 is an excerpt from the familiar account of the breakfast Jesus prepared for his disciples beside the Sea of Galilee after his Resurrection. In the story, Jesus commands Peter: "Feed my lambs. Tend my sheep." This was Jesus' way of telling Peter that those who love him must care for those in need, just as a shepherd cares for the flock.

Hymn: "There Is a Need for Shepherds" (SHEP-HERDS TODAY)

Text: The text, inspired by John 21:15-17 and a poem by Manfred Carter, was written by Mary Nelson Keithahn in 1992. It was the last song in a musical drama that traced the concept of shepherds in the Bible and pointed out the need for Christians to be responsible shepherds, not only where they live but throughout the world. The clear, simple language of the text makes it easily understood by children of all ages.

Tune: John D. Horman adapted the tune from the anthem version he wrote for the musical drama, and named it SHEPHERDS TODAY after the theme of the text.

Preparation

- Reproduce the hymn pages for each child.
- Cut out the Shepherd Riddle Cards. If you plan to reuse this session, you may want to laminate them for durability.
- Gather hats and props to represent the occupations mentioned on the Shepherd Riddle Cards.
- Prepare the banner backing by turning under 1/2-inch hems at the side and a one-inch casing at the top. Fringe or hem the bottom edge, depending on the type of fabric used. Insert the dowel after the design is applied.
- Mark Bibles with the scripture references the children will read.
- Learn the new hymn.
- Choose a helping organization in the community (e.g., retirement home, hospital unit, homeless shelter, children's home) to receive the banner and invite a representative to come to the closing portion of the class. Ask this person to give a brief explanation of the organization to the children. Invite the pastor to be present also, and to offer a closing prayer.
- Optional: Copy page 90 for a take-home coloring page (one per child).

The Session

1. Playing "Name that Tune" and Learning a Song About Shepherds. As the children gather, play familiar tunes such as "Jesus Loves Me," "Twinkle, Twinkle, Little Star," and "Jingle Bells" for them to name. Start by playing the first two pitches of a tune on the piano, then three, and so on until the children have guessed the correct name. One of the children may

Shepherds Live Around Us

Shep - herds all a - round us, here and ev - ery - where.
Help - ing those who need them, show - ing us they care.
You may know each shep - herd by a dif - ferent name,
but the love they of - fer al - ways is the same.

WORDS: John D. Horman
MUSIC: Traditional French melody
© 2000 Abingdon Press

know a song to play as well. Make your last tune "Au Clair de la Lune" (see page 15). Some of the children may recognize it from their piano lessons or from the children's hymn, "Jesus' Hands Were Kind Hands." Explain that "Shepherds Live Around Us" is also sung to this tune. Sing it a phrase at a time, asking the children to sing the words after you. Ask if any child knows how to play the tune on the piano. Have the others sing the new text as the child plays. *(Ten minutes)*

2. Discussing Two Passages of Scripture. If you made a list of things shepherds do in Session 1-A, review that with the group. If not, invite the children to share what they know. Have one of the older children read Ezekiel 34:15-16, using the Bible you marked previously. Ask: "Who is speaking? What are five things God says the shepherd will do for the sheep?" Compare those with the earlier list.

Explain that Jesus talked to his friends about their work as shepherds when he cooked breakfast for them beside the sea after his Resurrection. Let another older child read about this conversation as recorded in John 21:15-17. Ask: "What do you think Jesus was trying to tell Peter?" Comment that Peter carried on the work of the Good Shepherd. He told people about Jesus. He healed people who were sick. He welcomed strangers who wanted to be followers of Jesus too.

3. Solving Some Riddles. Have the Shepherd Riddle Cards, and hats and props representing different occupations ready. Explain: "There are people like Peter today who carry on the work of Jesus, the Good Shepherd. Let's see if we can guess who some of them are."

Let children take turns reading one of the eight riddles, and tell the others to raise their hands if they want to guess the speaker's identity. Choose one child to answer and another to find the appropriate hat and prop for the speaker to wear.

When you have identified all the "shepherds," invite the children to suggest ways that they too can show their love for Jesus by being shepherds (e.g., being kind to parents, feeding the dog, hugging a grandparent, picking up trash in the street, bringing a can of food for the food shelf, helping to plant a tree). *(Eight to ten minutes)*

4. Making a "Shepherds Today" Banner. Move to the art center. Trace each child's hand on a piece of felt in a skin tone the child has chosen. Carefully cut out the felt "hands." As you work, remind the children of ways that shepherds in the Bible used their hands to help the sheep. Then help them identify their shepherding "gifts." Some examples of ways they can "give a hand" to help others include: a flower for a sick friend, a book to share with a sibling, a broom for sweeping up spills on the kitchen floor, a heart for a hug, a get-well card, a recycling bin for cans, a dog on a leash, a snow shovel. Suggest that they each create a symbol for a particular gift, using felt scraps decorated with the puffy and glitter paint, and glue it onto their felt hands.

On another table, lay out the prepared banner. (Note: If you have used burlap as a banner backing, put wax paper underneath it to catch any glue that may soak through the fabric.) While the "hands" dry, give each child a letter

THERE IS A NEED FOR SHEPHERDS IN OUR WORLD

Shepherd Riddle Cards
(to be cut apart)

I am a shepherd.
Do you know me?
I grow the food
for your family.

I am a shepherd.
Do you know me?
I'm trained how to fight
to keep you all free.

I am a shepherd.
Do you know me?
When you are sick,
you come to see me.

I am a shepherd.
Do you know me?
I gather your food
from the deep blue sea.

I am a shepherd.
Who else am I?
I mix the batter
for bread, cake, and pie.

I am a shepherd.
Do you know me?
I tell of God's love
for you and for me.

I am a shepherd.
Do you know me?
I lead the country
from Washington, D.C.

I am a shepherd.
Who else am I?
I help you learn who, what,
where, when, and why.

I am a shepherd.
Do you know me?
I care for your teeth
when you come visit me.

I am a shepherd.
Who else am I?
I see that you're safe
and am always nearby.

I am a shepherd
Who else am I?
I work to save lives
when there's smoke in the sky.

I am a shepherd.
Who else am I?
I build the houses
that you occupy.

to glue on the banner for the title, "There Is a Need for Shepherds in Our World." (See page 16.) Then help them glue their hands on the banner below the words. Be sure that all the pieces are securely fastened so that they will not droop or fall off later. When the banner is dry, use the yarn needle to insert strands of yarn at four-inch intervals across the top of the banner. Use the yarn to tie the banner loosely to the dowel. Attach the cord, and hang the banner on the wall for presentation later.

While you work, talk with the children informally about the purpose of the organization that will receive the banner and how it might help them (e.g., by reminding them that people care for them, encouraging conversation about ways they can care for one another, adding a cheerful, happy wall hanging to their space). *(Fifteen minutes)*

5. Learning the Hymn. Gather the children around the piano and pass out copies of the hymn, "There Is a Need for Shepherds." Have them look at the tune name (SHEPHERDS TODAY). Ask: "What do you think this hymn is about?" Teach the refrain first. The refrain has two phrases or musical ideas. Sing each one, asking the children to echo you until they can sing the whole refrain with confidence. Then sing the first stanza alone, inviting the children to join in on the refrain when it occurs.

Ask the children if they hear any part of the refrain in the stanza of the hymn. (The first lines match.) Instruct them to sing on the first phrase of the stanza also. Ask if the tune to the stanza stays in the same place or moves up or down. (It rises.) Continue singing the stanzas, encouraging the children to sing more and more on each one.

As the children become comfortable with the hymn, discuss each stanza, pointing out any words or phrases that need explanation. After singing the hymn all the way through, talk about how the music and text make the children feel. Help them identify the areas of need depicted in each stanza. Ask: "What does the last phrase mean: 'There is a need for Love to show its power'? Why is the word *Love* capitalized? How does the last line relate to what Jesus said to Peter in the scripture we read earlier?" *(Sixteen to eighteen minutes)*

6. Sharing the Banner and a Prayer. As the children finish singing, welcome your pastor and the representative of the organization chosen to receive the banner. After the representative tells the children a little about the organization, encourage the children to explain their banner and the symbols in each hand. If there is time, sing one or two stanzas of "There Is a Need for Shepherds" before the pastor offers the closing prayer. *(Seven to ten minutes)*

Note: If you plan to use the hymn sing at the end of the course, you may want to delay presentation of the banner or arrange to borrow it so you can display it in the worship area for that service.

Questions for Reflection————

- In what way did the hymn assist children in identifying areas of need in today's world?
- How has this session helped children begin to discover ways they can be shepherds today?
- How did the art project teach the children new ways of helping others?

 # Who Is Jesus?
Our Advocate

Something Old: "Tell Me the Stories of Jesus"

Purpose: To help the children discover that Jesus was an advocate for the children who came to see him.

Objectives: By the end of the session the children may be able to:
1. Retell Matthew 19:13-15 in their own words.
2. Sing the first stanza of the hymn "Tell Me the Stories of Jesus."
3. Define the word *advocate* as it relates to the story.
4. Explain that one of Jesus' roles was as an advocate for children.

Materials Needed
- Bible
- Copies of the hymn (page 70)
- Piano
- Ten-inch balloons in various colors
- Large plastic trash bag
- Name tags and markers (optional)
- Template from book
- One sheet of heavyweight black paper for each child
- White pencil
- Tissue paper in assorted colors
- Scissors
- White glue
- Transparent tape

Background for the Leader

Scripture: Matthew 19:13-15

These three verses, which also appear in Mark and Luke, record one of the few incidents in the Gospels involving children. Jesus has left the Galilee and journeyed to an area of Judea close to the Jordan river. People have gathered to hear him teach and preach about marriage and divorce. Parents who have come with their children want Jesus to bless them. As adults so often do, the busy disciples treat the children as unimportant and turn them away. Jesus, however, recognizing the innocent faith and trusting love of the children, welcomes them and blesses them. He is an "advocate" for the children.

Hymn: "Tell Me the Stories of Jesus" (STORIES OF JESUS)

Text: William H. Parker, a Sunday school teacher at Chelsea Street Baptist Church in Nottingham, England, must have been a fine storyteller and poet. One day, when his students begged, "Teacher, tell us another story," he answered their request with this text about the life and ministry of Jesus. Originally it had six stanzas, which were printed on a hymn sheet and included in the *Sunday School Hymnary* published in 1905. The stanzas about Jesus' miracles and passion were later deleted because Christian educators thought them beyond the children's comprehension.

Tune: STORIES OF JESUS was a prize-winning tune in a 1903 centennial competition sponsored by the national Sunday School Union in London. It won acclaim from Frederick Bridge, organist at Westminster Abbey and judge of the contest, who said: "This is the best. A fine hymn too. In a few years it will be sung all over the kingdom." The tune, written by Frederick A. Challinor, was first published with the text in the *Sunday School Hymnal*, 1905.

Preparation

- Blow up and tie balloons, one for each child. Keep the balloons in a large plastic trash bag.
- Gather the art supplies.
- Trace the template design for the stained glass windows onto black paper with a white pencil (page 21). Carefully cut out all the shaded spaces. Prepare one sheet for each child.
- Make enough copies of the hymn for each child.
- Optional: Copy page 91 for a take-home coloring page (one per child)

The Session

1. Sharing a Story. As the children come in, have everyone make a name tag, and come into the story circle. Greet each child warmly. Ask the children to tell you their names and their favorite story about Jesus or a story that Jesus told. *(Five minutes)*

2. Exploring the Scripture. Open the Bible to Matthew 19:13-15 and tell the children you are going to share one of your favorite stories about Jesus, one that they may have heard before. Read the scripture, and then comment: "The mood of this story is serious and sad at first. Think how the children must have felt when the disciples tried to chase them away. Imagine how stern the men's voices must have sounded to them! But then, something wonderful happened to lighten their mood. What was it?" Wait for them to tell about Jesus' invitation to the children. Continue: "How did the children feel then? Let's see if we can share their light and joyful mood as we learn a hymn about the story." *(Five minutes)*

3. Learning the Hymn. Give each child a balloon and ask them to stand in different places around the room. Show them how to bounce the balloons in the air on their fingertips, and let them practice. Explain that the piano will play one phrase at a time. Instruct them to bounce their balloons on the two strong pulses in each measure of the 6/8 time, and then hold the balloons to their chests and listen as the phrase is repeated. For example:

```
*     *     *   *   *    *    *     X
```
Tell me the sto-ries of Je-sus, I want to hear. . . .

(* = bounce balloon; X = hold balloon to chest)

While the children are still holding their balloons, ask them to listen as you sing the words in a light, cheerful style suggested by the bouncing balloons. Then have them echo-sing the phrase back to you. Repeat this procedure for each phrase until you have sung through the first stanza. Do the same for stanza 2. Have the children put the balloons back in the trash bag. Then hand out photocopies of the hymn and sing the first two stanzas together. *(Twenty minutes)*

4. Identifying Jesus as an Advocate. Have the children look at the second stanza of the hymn. Ask: "Where do you think the poet got the idea for this stanza?" Read the passage from Matthew again. Comment: "Jesus was acting as an 'advocate' for children in this story." *(Write the word on the chalkboard or a chart.)* Continue: "Have you ever heard that word before? The dictionary says an advocate is someone who speaks on behalf of another person; someone who supports, defends, or recommends another publicly." Ask: "How did Jesus act as an advocate? What did he say to the other adults about the children? Do you think Jesus would be a good person to have on your side? Why?" *(Seven minutes)*

5. Making a "Stained Glass" Story Picture. Move over to the art table. Introduce the project with this comment: "Have you ever wondered why churches have stained glass windows? Long ago, Bibles were very expensive and not many people could read, so artists created pictures in stained glass to tell Bible stories. These windows were like their schoolbooks. We're going to tell the Bible story we read today in a 'stained glass' picture."

Give each child a prepared template sheet. Let the children choose different shades of colored tissue paper for each cutout section, working with one section at a time. Help them cut the tissue paper roughly to size. Line the back of the black frame section with a thin line of glue. Place the tissue paper over the opening and press it down carefully. Trim off excess tissue. Continue to cover each opening with colored tissue. When the picture is dry, turn it over and use a loop of transparent tape to hang it up in a sunny window, with the back side to the glass. *(Twenty minutes)*

6. Offering a Prayer. Gather the children together and pray: "Dear God, we are glad that Jesus told so many stories. We love to hear them, just as the children did so long ago. Thank you for helping Jesus be an advocate for them so they would not be turned away. We know Jesus is still speaking for children through all the people who care about us *(you might name several who are known to the children).* Help us remember to thank them. Amen." *(Three minutes)*

Questions for Reflection————————

- How did bouncing balloons affect the mood of the hymn learned today?
- Why is establishing that mood important to this hymn and the children's perception of Jesus?
- What did you see and hear to indicate that the children understood Jesus as their advocate?

2-B Who Is Jesus? Our Advocate

Something New: "The People Came from Everywhere"

Purpose: To help children identify Jesus as an advocate for the children who knew him, and relate that concept to the experiences of children today.

Objectives: By the end of the session the children may be able to:
1. Define the word *advocate* in their own words.
2. Sing two stanzas of a new hymn, "The People Came from Everywhere."
3. Recall the biblical story told in the hymn.
4. Identify Jesus as an advocate for children in that story.
5. Tell about people they know who are advocates for children.

Materials Needed
- Bible
- Copies of hymn (page 71)
- Chart board
- Extra-wide black marker
- Markers
- Pattern for Jesus (page 26)
- Overhead projector
- Pictures cut from magazines of people who help children
- Glue sticks
- Scissors
- 22" x 28" posterboard

Background for the Leader

Scripture: Mark 10:13-16

This incident is also recorded in Matthew (see Session 2-A) and Luke. News has spread that Jesus can heal by his touch, and parents have brought their children for him to touch so they too will receive his blessing. The disciples are annoyed at this interruption, and try to send them away. Jesus is indignant because the disciples are interfering with the manifestation of God's love.

Here Mark inserts another idea, perhaps drawn from earlier sayings of Jesus: People must receive the kingdom of God with the simple trust of a child. The faith of children is a model for adults to follow. Mark suggests that Jesus is not only an advocate for the children,

he also empowers the children to be advocates for adults.

That said, Mark finishes the story. Jesus takes the children in his arms and blesses them with his touch and his love.

Hymn: "The People Came from Everywhere" (CHILD'S PLAY)

Text: When Mary Nelson Keithahn decided to use Mark's account of Jesus and the children as the basis for a sermon, the only hymns she could find on the story were children's hymns. She decided Mark's text deserved a new hymn that the whole congregation could sing, and wrote "The People Came from Everywhere."

The hymn, like the scripture, combines Jesus' warm welcome to the children with a serious and important message for adults.

Tune: John Horman was thinking of the joyful, playful nature of children when he wrote the tune CHILD'S PLAY. He wanted people to remember how Jesus loved, valued, and accepted children.

Preparation

- Write the word ADVOCATE vertically in the center of a piece of chart paper.
- Write the dictionary definition of advocate (someone who speaks on behalf of another person, someone who supports, defends, or recommends another publicly) on another piece of chart paper.
- Become familiar with the hymn and the movement on the last phrase.

- Gather the art supplies.
- Using an overhead projector, project the illustration of Jesus found in the lesson onto the large sheet of posterboard and trace it with the thick felt-tip pen. (Or use a grid system to enlarge the drawing.) Cut out the image.
- Clip a large number of pictures of people helping children from magazines.

The Session

1. Defining the Word *Advocate* in an Acrostic. Have the children gather around the chart board where you have written the word *advocate* vertically on the paper. Post the definition chart on the wall where all can see it. Ask the children to help you think of other action words that tell what an advocate does and add them to the chart. Then work together to create an acrostic for the word *advocate* by writing one or more of these words next to each letter. For example:

> **A**cts, asks, acknowledges, addresses, argues
> **D**efends, decides, declares, debates
> **V**alues, voices
> **O**ffers, organizes, opens
> **C**hampions, cares, credits, coaxes
> **A**cclaims, assures, acquaints, appreciates
> **T**alks, teaches, tries
> **E**ncourages, educates, endeavors
> *(Five minutes)*

2. Learning the Hymn. Ask the children to count off by twos. Tell them to move away from one another, and find a spot on which to stand, using all the space in the room. Explain that they may travel anywhere they want in the room as long as they respect the other children's space and avoid touching any objects in the room. Have all the "1's" skip away from their starting places as you play and sing the first sentence of the text (ending with the word *news*). Have them skip back again on the second sentence (ending with the word *views*). In like manner, ask the "2's" to skip out and back on the third and fourth musical phrases. Then show the children how to add movement on the extension of the last phrase as follows:

	Snap	Clap	Pat	Right Stamp		Left Stamp
Don't	*both*	*—*	*er*	*him*	*to* —	*day.*

Sing and play each phrase of the hymn again, one line at a time, for the children to echo in song and movement. Then gather the children in a circle, hand out photocopies of the hymn, and sing stanzas 1 and 2 straight through together. *(Twenty minutes)*

3. Talking About the Bible Story. Ask: "What story does this hymn tell? Where is it found?" Explain that the story can be found in three places: Matthew, Mark, and Luke. The woman who wrote the text used Mark's account.

Have one of the older children read Mark 10:13-16. Help the children recall their definition of the word *advocate*. Comment: "If this incident had happened today, people would call Jesus an advocate for children. He argued publicly that children are important and that he wanted them to come to him. And when he pointed out that grown-ups must be as trusting as children to receive the gift of faith, Jesus showed that children could act as advocates too."

Then ask: "Who has been an advocate for you? What did they do? When have you had an opportunity to act as an advocate for others?" Share stories, if there is time. *(Ten minutes)*

4. Creating an Advocate Collage. Have the children move to the art table where you have laid out the magazine pictures you collected. Encourage the children to talk about people who have been advocates for them, and let them choose pictures that remind them of these experiences. Help the children cut out the people in their illustrations and glue them to the posterboard, touching and overlapping, until the whole figure is covered. Be more concerned with the children's grasp of the concept and enthusiasm for their advocates than with how neatly they cut the pictures. When the figure is covered, trim away the excess paper so the original shape of Jesus is revealed.

Use the completed collage to help the children recall all the people who have helped them by being their advocates. Comment: "Do you know why we made this picture in the shape of Jesus? This is the way God works. God puts the spirit of Jesus in our hearts so we will be advocates for one another." *(Twenty minutes)*

Note: If you are planning to use the hymn sing (Session Seven) save the Advocate Collage to display then.

5. Ending with Prayer. Have the children gather in a circle around the Advocate Collage. Explain: "Let's thank God now for people who have been our advocates. Close your eyes for a few seconds and think of someone who has spoken up for you. Then we'll go around the circle and everyone who wants to thank God for an advocate can have a turn. I'll start."

Let your prayer be a model for them to follow. For example: "Thank you, God, for Tom who recommended me as someone who could teach these children." Children may offer a prayer such as "Thank you, God, for my mother who talked to my teacher about my homework assignment."

When all have had a chance to speak or pass, close the prayer in this way: "Thank you, God, for giving us Jesus to speak for children

and their needs. Show us how to be advocates too. Amen." *(Five minutes)*

Questions for Reflection————

- Were the children easily able to find pictures of advocates in those you provided for the art activity?
- In what ways did the children show they understood the meaning of the word *advocate*?
- How does your church identify and help children who need extra support?
- What ways does your church provide opportunities for children to experience advocacy in action?

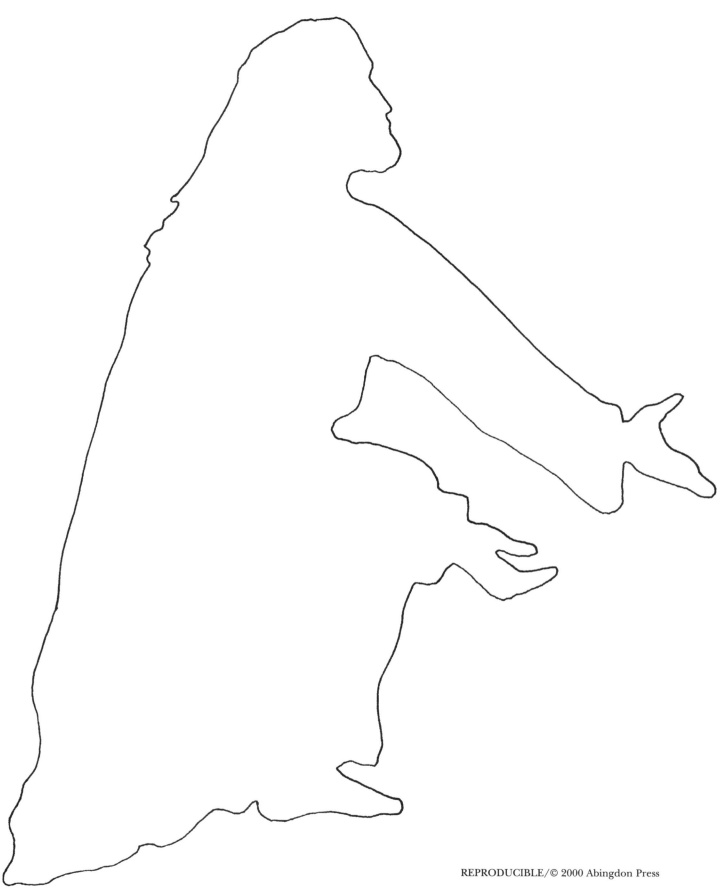

 # Who Is Jesus?
Our Way to God

Something Old: "Sweet Hour of Prayer"

Purpose: To help children learn from the example of Jesus that prayer is a way to communicate with God.

Objectives: By the end of the session the children may be able to:
1. Follow the tune of "Sweet Hour of Prayer" on a scale ladder.
2. Sing the first stanza of "Sweet Hour of Prayer."
3. Understand that Jesus took time to pray alone and with his friends.
4. Compose a simple prayer.

Materials Needed
- Bible
- Copies of the hymn (page 73)
- Piano or keyboard
- Chart board
- Markers
- Paper punch
- Copies of the "prayer ladder" worksheet (page 29)
- Two fairly straight sticks (e.g., saplings) about six feet long
- Eight smaller sticks about twelve inches long
- Material for lashing: Either twenty-inch lengths of leather laces or woven fabric cut in 3/4-inch strips, enough to lash the eight cross pieces to the ladder poles; one length per child
- Pony beads in mixed colors, with large enough holes to string on the leather laces or fabric
- Camel bells (one for each child)
- Natural materials such as feathers, dried flowers, or small pine cones for children to use in decorating the ladder
- Brown paper bags

Background for the Leader

Scripture: Mark 6:30-32, 45-46

Jesus knew that taking time away from the busy world to rest and talk with God in prayer gave him the strength he needed to teach, preach, heal, and carry on the other activities of his ministry. Sometimes he took his disciples with him, and sometimes he went alone, as is evident in Mark's "bookends" for his version of the feeding of the five thousand. Mark sets this miracle in the "deserted place" where Jesus retreated with his disciples for rest and prayer, only to be followed there by a multitude of persons wanting to be taught and healed. Once the five thousand were fed, Mark notes, Jesus sent the disciples on to the other shore, and went up on the mountain to pray alone.

Jesus' approach to prayer provides a model for our own prayer life. We all need to take time out from our busy lives to be with God, sometimes praying with others and sometimes praying alone. It is in such communal and private prayer that we find strength to be faithful disciples in today's world.

Hymn: "Sweet Hour of Prayer" (SWEET HOUR)

Text: It has long been thought that William W. Walford, a little-known blind lay preacher and owner of a trinket shop in the village of Colehill, Warwickshire, England, wrote this beloved hymn. His friend, Thomas Salmon, claimed to have heard the poet recite his newly written stanzas when he visited him in 1842. Salmon carried a written copy of the hymn with him to the United States. There he showed it to an editor of the *New York Observer,* who published the poem for the first time in the September 13, 1845 issue. The authorship of this text was questioned in 1964 by William Reynolds in his book, *Hymns of Our Faith.* He reported he had been unable to verify that a William W. Walford lived in Colehill in 1842, and attributed the hymn instead to the Rev. William Walford, a Congregational minister who wrote many books on the subject of prayer. However, he also suggested that the two Walfords could have been the same man.

Tune: The tune SWEET HOUR was written in 1861 by William Batchelder Bradbury, an American composer of early gospel music. The text and tune first appeared together in *Golden Chain,* a hymnal collection published that same year.

Preparation

- Make copies of the hymn and the prayer ladder worksheet for each child.
- Enlarge a copy of the prayer ladder for the display board so it can be used for writing a group prayer.
- Gather art supplies.

- Cut free-form shapes from the paper bags for the children to use in illustrating/writing their prayers to tie on the ladder. Punch a hole in the top of each.

The Session

1. Making a Ladder. Have the sticks laid out on the floor in the shape of a ladder when the children arrive. Ask: "Who can guess what we're going to make today?" When they have identified the ladder, continue: "Why do we use ladders? What is their purpose?" Let the children talk about how we use ladders to help us reach something beyond our physical limits. Suggest that prayer is like a ladder. It helps us reach God.

Give each of the children a leather lace or strip of fabric and show them how to lash the smaller sticks between the longer poles like rungs on a ladder. If there are more than sixteen children, let them tie more than one lace or cloth strip to a joint. Ask them to leave about ten inches of their lace or cloth strip hanging freely so that they can string pony beads on it, leaving space at the end to add other decorations.

Give each child a brown paper shape. Explain that in the modern State of Israel people often write prayers on small slips of paper to place in the cracks of the "Wailing Wall" in Jerusalem when they want to talk to God. Suggest that the children think about something they want to tell or ask God and provide felt-tip pens, crayons, or paints for them to use in illustrating that prayer. (You may need to provide some simple examples: a heart for "I love you, God" or "I pray for love"; a cloud with rain for "Please send us rain"; a sad face for "Please help my friend who is sad because his grandpa is sick.") Then have them tie their prayers on their laces below the beads, and secure them in place with small camel bells. Those who finish first can add other decorations to the ladder such as feathers, dried flowers, or small pine cones. *(Fifteen minutes)*

2. Describing a Scale as a "Musical Ladder." Gather the children around the piano. Write *la scala* on a chalkboard and tell the children it is the word for "ladder" in Italian. Comment that there is a famous opera house in Italy called La Scala. Ask: "Why do you think Italians gave this name to a place where they go to hear people

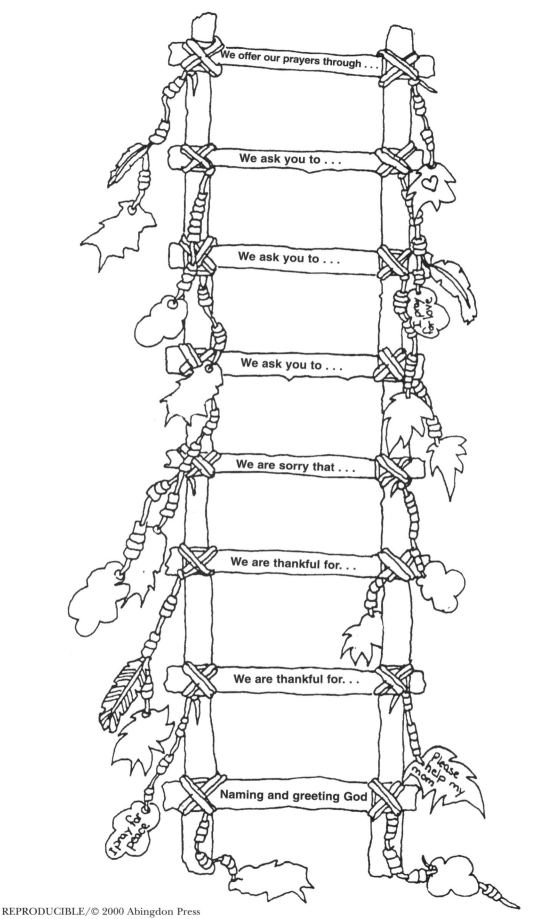

We offer our prayers through . . .

We ask you to . . .

We ask you to . . .

We ask you to . . .

We are sorry that . . .

We are thankful for. . .

We are thankful for. . .

Naming and greeting God

I love you

I pray for peace

Please help my mom

sing? What does a ladder have to do with singing?" If the children do not come up with the idea of the "scale" right away, ask them to think of a "musical ladder" and talk about how we sing up and down a scale like the steps of a ladder.

3. Learning the Hymn. Direct the children's attention to the ladder so that you can use the "steps" to illustrate the upward and downward motion of the melody line.

Sing the ascending first half of the first phrase, using a number for each pitch and pointing to each note in the scale as it's sung. Have the children sing it back to you, again pointing to each note and calling their attention to the tone that is skipped (the second).

Sing the second half of the first phrase in the same way for the children to echo. Then ask: "What direction does the phrase move, up or down? Does the second tone of the scale get used this time?" (Yes)

Use this approach to teach the rest of the stanza a phrase at a time. When you have sung through the hymn together in this way, have the children count the number of phrases and determine which of the four are most alike. They should quickly identify that the third phrase is different, and that the others are alike. Pass out photocopies of the hymn and sing stanza 1 all the way through, following the text and tune with index fingers as you sing. *(Twenty minutes)*

4. Discussing a Bible Story. Introduce the story with reference to the hymn: "We have just sung a hymn about prayer. What is a prayer?" As they share their ideas, help them focus on prayer as a way of talking with God. Then ask: "How is prayer like a ladder?" If they are unable to make the connection, suggest that a ladder helps us go where we need to be and farther than we can physically go ourselves. Explain that prayer was the ladder Jesus used when he wanted to get in touch with God.

Open the Bible to Mark 6, and comment: "The sixth chapter of Mark tells about two times when Jesus stopped what he was doing to pray. Listen carefully, and see if you can figure out who was with Jesus each time."

Read Mark 6:30-32. Give the children a chance to share what they discovered and then comment: "Jesus knew the disciples had been busy and needed some time to be quiet and talk with God. He wanted them to learn how important it was to find time to pray."

Read Mark 6:45-46 and ask: "Who was with Jesus this time?" Allow time for the children to respond, and then continue: "Jesus often prayed with his friends, but sometimes he needed to pray alone. He wanted the disciples to learn that they could pray at any time, in any place, with anyone or by themselves."

Ask: "When are some times that you pray with others? When do you need to pray alone?" Encourage the children to think about prayers with others in morning worship and church school, at the dinner table, and with the family at bedtime; and solitary prayers when they feel alone, frightened, angry, sad, or worried (or thankful and happy). *(Ten minutes)*

5. Writing a Prayer Together. Have the children sit in a circle around the ladder. Direct their attention to the ladder on the display board. Explain: "Here is another kind of ladder that can help us learn the steps in writing a prayer. We'll start at the bottom, and by the time we reach the top rung we will have a prayer to offer to God." Work on a group prayer, using the prayer ladder as a guide. Record the prayer on the chart board. For example:

Rung 1: Naming and greeting God
(Gracious God, we love you).

Rungs 2-3: We are thankful for . . .
(this beautiful day, our families, our friends at church).

Rung 4: We are sorry that . . .
(we were unkind to our friends).

Rungs 5-7: We ask you to . . .
(take care of children everywhere, protect our loved ones, help Tommy's grandma get well).

Rung 8: We offer our prayers through *(our Lord Jesus Christ. Amen.)*

Note: If you plan to use the hymn sing at the end of the course, you may want to save a copy of the group prayer to include in the service and use the prayer ladder in the worship area. *(Ten minutes)*

6. Ending with the Prayer. Have the children stand in a circle, holding hands, and pray the group prayer they have written together. Before the children leave, give them copies of the prayer ladder to take home. Explain that they can use the ladder as a guide for prayers with their families. Suggest that they post the ladder where the family gathers for meals, so they can take a few minutes to "climb the ladder" together; or display the ladder in their own rooms as a guide to prayer at bedtime. *(Five minutes)*

Questions for Reflection————————

- How effective was the ladder as an illustration for teaching the function of prayer in Jesus' life and ours?
- How was the ladder helpful in teaching the hymn?
- Did the children seem comfortable with writing a prayer?
- How can we encourage families to use the prayer ladders as a guide to informal prayer at home?

3-B Who Is Jesus? Our Way to God

Something New: "Come Away with Me"

Purpose: To help children follow the example of Jesus in finding time apart from their scheduled lives to experience God through prayer.

Objectives: By the end of the session the children may be able to:
1. Talk about the importance of quiet times in their daily lives.
2. Identify times in the Bible when Jesus drew near to God through prayer.
3. Sing the first two stanzas of the hymn, "Come Away with Me."

Materials Needed
- Bibles
- Copies of the hymn (page 74)
- Piano or keyboard
- Chart board
- Markers
- Nine-inch-long colored mailing tubes (one for each child)

- Various "quiet" objects, such as feathers, shells, precut felt butterflies, white batting (for clouds), pompoms (for caterpillars), stickers (fish, hearts, stars, rainbows, snowflakes), silk leaves (enough for the children to have a variety from which to choose)
- Paper lunch bags, or zip-top bags
- Glue

Background for the Leader

Scripture: Mark 6:30-32; Matthew 14:13; 6:6; 26:36

Jesus was in the Galilee when he received news that John the Baptist had been killed. His cousin's death must have caused him great pain and sorrow, for he immediately withdrew from his work to pray. According to Mark, he invited his disciples to go with him, but in Matthew's account, he went alone. As often happened during his ministry, large crowds followed him wherever he went. Like all of us today, it was difficult for Jesus to find time to pray.

The three excerpts from the Gospel of Matthew tell us that sometimes Jesus went off by himself in a boat on the Sea of Galilee to pray alone. Sometimes he prayed surrounded by

people on a hillside above the sea. And at the end, he prayed alone in the Garden of Gethsemane after the Passover meal, bidding his disciples sit apart from him to keep watch. No matter where he was, Jesus turned to prayer as a way to experience the presence of God.

Hymn: "Come Away with Me" (RECREATION)

Text: Mary Nelson Keithahn had been asked by a friend to write a text for a children's anthem on Mark 6:30-32. While working on that assignment, she awoke one morning with the first two stanzas of "Come Away with Me" in her head. She felt compelled to put aside the anthem text until she finished the hymn. "Come Away with

Me" is an invitation to prayer, and makes reference to the acts of thanksgiving, praise, confession and absolution that are a part of the prayer experience. The second stanza draws on the references in Matthew to times when Jesus prayed in places that had spiritual significance for the poet when she visited the Holy Land.

Tune: John Horman named his tune RECREATION because it is through rest, relaxation, and prayer that we experience God's presence and are "re-created" to begin God's work anew.

Preparation

- Mark Bibles with the references from Matthew.
- Make copies of the hymn.
- Gather the art supplies.
- Plan the quiet walk.

The Session

1. Talking About Prayer. Gather the children at the piano as they arrive. Encourage them to talk about their daily schedules. Ask: "With such busy schedules, when do children find time to pray?" Let them share their experiences about when, where, and why they pray. Comment: "People talk with God at different times, in different places, for different reasons." *(Continue talking about the different ways people pray, demonstrating each one for the children to imitate.)*

"Some people stand, some sit, and some kneel to pray. Some people lift up their hands and heads, some put their palms together or fold their hands and bow their heads, and others join hands with their neighbors. Some people pray silently or whisper their prayers so that only God can hear them; others pray aloud alone or with a group. No matter how or when or where we talk to God, we know God listens to us. But how do we listen to God?" *(Pause to let them answer, and then continue.)*

"We listen to God by being quiet. Try being very still. Close your eyes and be perfectly quiet for thirty seconds. Have a quiet conversation with God." *(Ten minutes)*

2. Learning the Hymn by Playing a Game. At the end of the thirty seconds begin playing "Come Away with Me" on the piano while an assistant passes out copies of the hymn to each child. Teach the hymn by singing it one phrase at a time for the children to echo. Once you have sung the first two stanzas of the hymn in this manner, sing them over again without the children, stopping at different points in each stanza. Instruct the children to follow the hymn on their copies, tracing the words and melody with their index fingers as they "think" the tune. Tell them that when you stop singing, they are to say or sing the next word of the phrase. Each time you stop, return to the beginning of that stanza until you have completely made your way through both stanzas of the hymn.

Note: If some in the group have limited reading skills, use the buddy system and pair these children with older, more secure children. *(Ten minutes)*

3. Reading Some Bible Verses. Read Mark 6:30-32. Ask: "How is the hymn like the Bible verse?" After they have shared their ideas, have different children read Matthew 14:13; 6:6; and 26:36. Ask the children to find the places mentioned in each passage in the second stanza of the hymn (in a boat on a gentle sea, on the hillside where Jesus preached the Sermon on the Mount, and in the Garden of Gethsemane). *(Five minutes)*

4. Creating "Quiet Boxes." Move to the art center. Let each child choose a colored tube and remove the plastic top. *(Have them save the tops to use later)*. Help the children select and glue quiet objects to the outside of their tubes. While the tubes are drying, take the children on the "listening walk." *(Ten minutes)*

5. Going on a "Listening Walk." Give each child a small plastic sandwich bag. Explain: "We are going on a short walk outside to listen to the quiet. While we are there you can pick up items of nature that remind you of quiet times with God and put them in your bag. We will all need to walk quietly, and sometimes even stop and stand very still to listen." *(Fifteen minutes)*

6. Whispering a Prayer. Return to the art center with the children. Ask: "How did it feel

to be very quiet? What sounds did we hear on our 'listening walk'? Were they noisy sounds or quiet sounds? What would we have missed if we had been talking out loud?" Comment: "It's important to find a quiet time each day to hear our own thoughts and God's thoughts."

Tell the children they can put the items they collected on their walk in their "quiet boxes" now. Suggest that before they put the lid on their tube that they whisper into it one thing that they would like to share with God. It could be a word of thanks for something they found, a question it provoked, or some other quiet thought. Tell the children that they may open their "quiet boxes" at any time to help them remember their "listening walk" and the quiet thought they shared with God, and they can add more quiet thoughts as they want. Close with a full minute of silence, followed by an "Amen." *(Ten minutes)*

Questions for Reflection——

- How did being quiet help the children feel closer to God?
- In what ways were the children able to relate the objects found on the "listening walk" to God's presence?
- What mood was created by the hymn and how did it enhance the overall lesson?

 **Who Is Jesus?**
Our Leader
Something Old: "Jesus Calls Us O'er the Tumult"

Purpose: To help children explore what it means to be called by Jesus.

Objectives:
By the end of the session the children may be able to:
1. Tell the story of Jesus' call to the disciples in their own words.
2. Sing one stanza of the hymn, "Jesus Calls Us O'er the Tumult."
3. Identify the "tumult" in their lives that can interfere with Jesus' call to them.

Materials Needed
- Bible
- Copies of the hymn (page 75)
- Piano or keyboard
- Chart board
- Markers
- Compass
- Scissors
- Colored string
- Hole punch
- Blue posterboard, about an eight-inch square (one for each child)
- Brightly colored Japanese printed origami paper (heavier weight) cut in 1" x 6" strips (four for each child)
- Small bells that tinkle (four for each child)
- Colored construction paper (optional)
- Plain origami paper (optional)

Background for the Leader

Scripture: Matthew 4:18-22

When Jesus returned from his forty days in the Judean wilderness and heard that John the Baptist had been arrested, he went back to the Galilee and moved from his home town of Nazareth to the fishing village of Capernaum on the sea of Galilee. There he began his ministry. The Gospel of Matthew saw this as a fulfillment of Isaiah's prophecy about where the Messiah would be found.

One of Jesus' first steps was to call disciples to share in his ministry, as recorded in Matthew 4:18-22. The important word in this passage is "immediately" (the Greek word *eutheos*). The four fishermen left the "tumult of life's wild restless sea" and immediately followed Jesus.

They didn't think about it, or check with their parents, or ask if they could have the weekend to get ready. They went when they were called.

These men probably knew Jesus already, or had heard about him; James and John may have been related to Jesus through their mother. Peter and his family lived with Peter's mother-in-law who had a house in Capernaum, and it is thought that Jesus also stayed there on and off during his ministry. Andrew was Peter's brother and would have been acquainted with his friends. However, even if they knew Jesus before they heard his call, for them to follow Jesus "immediately" was nothing short of extraordinary.

Hymn: "Jesus Calls Us O'er the Tumult"
(GALILEE)

Text: Cecil F. Alexander, one of Great Britain's finest hymn writers, wrote this text about discipleship and commitment for her husband, a distinguished clergyman who eventually became archbishop of Ireland. The pastor used it in his sermon on St. Andrew's Day, traditionally an important day in the liturgical year for the Anglican Church. It celebrates the day that Jesus called the fisherman Andrew to be his disciple (Mark 1:16-18). St. Andrew is the patron saint of Scotland. The second stanza originally began "As of old, Saint Andrew heard it," but in some hymnals it has been edited to read "As of old the apostles heard it."

Tune: GALILEE was composed for this text by William Herbert Jude, who was born in 1851 in Westleton, Suffolk, England. Jude was an accomplished organist and the editor of several music publications. Although he wrote GALILEE in 1874, it did not appear with text until they were published together in *Congregational Church Hymns*, 1888.

Preparation

- Make copies of the hymn.
- Make a word chart for first stanza of the text.
- Gather the art supplies.
- Prepare each ring for the mobile as follows: (1) With the compass, draw an eight-inch circle on a piece of blue cardboard. Cut out this circle, and then draw another circle inside it about one inch smaller in diameter. Cut out this circle too, leaving an eight-inch ring. (2) Punch twelve evenly spaced holes around the ring. (3) Cut four 18-inch pieces of string and attach them to the holes at the quadrants of the ring. Tie the strings together at the other end to serve as the hanger for the mobile. (See page 37.) Make sure that the ring hangs level.
- Punch holes at the top and bottom of the origami paper strips.

The Session

1. Hearing a Call. As the children gather, ask: "Show me how your parents say your name when you're really little; when you have done something wrong; when they see you are in danger; or when they want you to come inside." After a few examples, say: "Sometimes moms and dads use our names in different ways. Sometimes they str   ar names out and add pitches to them, lik   _his." *(Sing examples below.)*

"Why do you think they do this? Has it anything to do with the way they feel? (Loving? Angry? Worried? Impatient?) How does the way they call your name affect you? How do your feelings affect the way you call someone's name?

Gathering Activity

Be - ver - ly,   Car - los,   Al - li - son,

Su - zi,   Mar - ga - ret,   John. _____

WORDS and MUSIC: John D. Horman
© 2000 Abingdon Press

"When you sing someone's name, how do you know which syllable of the name to make longer?" *(Repeat several examples from above.)* Accept their answers, and then comment: "The strong syllable of a name is the one we accent or sing louder than the others. Try singing your name that way." Give everyone who wants a chance to try. *(Five minutes)*

2. Learning the Song. Use a word chart for "Jesus Calls Us O'er the Tumult" to aid the children in singing the text clearly and expressively. Read through the text together and ask the children to help identify the important words (e.g., Jesus, calls, tumult, wild, Christian, follow) and talk about their meaning. *Tumult* may be a new word for the children. Explain that it means a noisy commotion, clamor, disorder, uproar, disturbance. Ask: "What kind of 'tumults' do children have in their lives that might make it hard for them to hear the call of Jesus?"

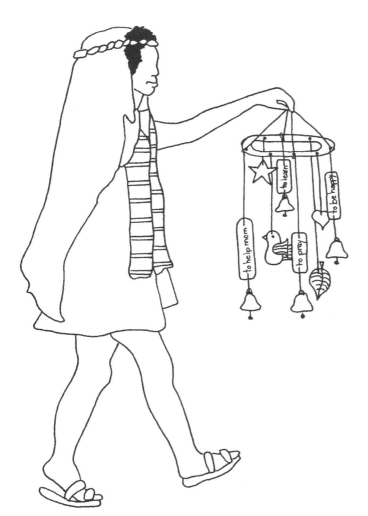

Underline the words you identified (see below), and explain that the important words in a song are usually accented (sung more loudly).

<u>Jesus calls</u> us o'er the <u>tumult</u>
of our life's <u>wild</u>, restless sea;
day by day his sweet voice soundeth,
saying, "<u>Christian, follow</u> me!"

Sing one phrase at a time for the children to sing back to you. Be careful to stress each underlined word. Then sing the whole stanza together. After the children feel secure with that, sing the stanza alone with the exception of the underlined words. Ask the children to sing those. This will require them to concentrate and focus on the text and tune in order to sing both the word and pitch correctly. When you have finished, ask: "If we didn't accent important words and syllables in a song, how would it sound? How do accented syllables help us understand the meaning of the words we sing?" Then pass out photocopies of the hymn and sing the first stanza again together. *(Fifteen minutes)*

3. Listening to a Bible Story. Open the Bible to Matthew 4:18-22 and introduce the story something like this: "Stories have important words too, and we accent those words when we speak. The important word in today's story is *immediately.* Who knows what that means?" Give them a chance to respond, and then ask them to listen carefully and raise their hands when they hear the word in the story. Read the passage from Matthew. Then ask: "Why is *immediately* an important word in this story?" Let them share their ideas, and then comment: "Peter and the other fishermen left their work and went immediately with Jesus. They didn't think about it or ask for time to make arrangements. Jesus must have been pretty special for them to leave everything behind and immediately go with him."

Suggest that the children act out the story. Choose four children to be James, John, Peter and Andrew, one to be Zebedee, and one to be Jesus. Ask: "How do you think the fishermen felt when they heard Jesus call? How did Zebedee feel when his sons went off with Jesus? How did Jesus feel when the four men came with him immediately?"

Ask the children if they know of anyone today whom Jesus has called to do something special. They may name the pastor, a church school teacher, or other adult. Be sure to add examples of young people who have felt called to do something very important; for example, a Baltimore teenager who started her own program for feeding homeless people, or young people who donated suitcases to foster children. Ask them to think about what Jesus might be calling them to do. *(Fifteen minutes)*

4. Constructing a "Windsong Mobile." Give each child one of the blue rings you have prepared earlier and the four strips of origami paper. Have the children write something that Jesus calls them to do on each strip (e.g., love God, tell others about Jesus, be a good friend, help others, show kindness). Then help them attach small bells with string to the bottom of each strip and attach each strip with string to the cardboard ring. If there is time, let the children draw and/or cut out shapes of flowers, stars, birds, hearts, leaves, or other objects to hang from the remaining holes in the ring. Have regular origami paper available for anyone who might like to fold a figure to add to the mobile. As you work together, talk about the sound they will hear when the wind blows through the mobile. Suggest that it will help

them remember what Jesus is calling them to do. *(Twenty minutes)*

Note: If you plan to use the hymn sing at the end of the course, you may want to arrange to keep one of the mobiles to display in the worship area for that service.

5. Sharing a Quiet Time for Prayer. Ask the children to be quiet for thirty seconds and then, when you give the signal, move their windsong mobiles so the bells will ring, reminding us that Jesus calls each of us to follow him in our own way. Close with a prayer: "Help us, God, to find a quiet time and place each day away from the tumult of our lives, so that we can talk with you and listen for our call to follow Jesus. Give us faith enough to say 'Yes.' Amen." *(Five minutes)*

Questions for Reflection——————
  • How did the children respond to the word "call"?
  • How crowded are their schedules? What are the other "tumults" in their lives? How do they feel about them?
  • How can we help children and their families find time in their lives to listen for the call of Jesus and respond?

4-B Who Is Jesus? Our Leader

Something New: "Jesus Sang to Fishermen"

Purpose: To help children discover that leaders must sometimes be followers too.

Objectives: By the end of the session the children may be able to:
1. Tell that the disciples were ordinary people who trusted Jesus enough to leave everything and follow him.
2. Sing the first stanza of "Jesus Sang to Fishermen."
3. Explain that followers of Jesus are willing to take turns at being leaders in the church, according to their special gifts.

Materials Needed
- Bible
- Drawing paper (one sheet for each child)
- Copies of the hymn (page 76)
- Piano or keyboard
- Fine-point tubes of glitter paint in various colors
- Chart board
- Brightly colored markers (several choices for each child)

Background for the Leader

Scripture: Matthew 4:18-22

The kind of people Jesus called to work side by side with him were not the very religious Pharisees and Sadducees. They were not the wealthiest or the most educated or the most important people. Jesus called his disciples from every walk of life. They were common, ordinary people who knew how to work hard and play hard, people who had suffered and done wrong things, people who trusted in the God who offered them love and forgiveness. In other words, the people Jesus called were just like us, which suggests that we can be his followers too. *(See also the Bible background in Session 4-A.)*

Hymn: "Jesus Sang to Fishermen" (BLACK MOUNTAIN)

Text: Mary Nelson Keithahn's text recalls the motley group of people who were among the first to answer the call of Jesus. The first stanza makes reference to the call of the fishermen recorded in Matthew 4:18-22. Other stanzas mention tax collectors (Matthew/Levi and Zacchaeus) and sinners (Mary Magdalene), persons considered unacceptable by the Jews (people with disabilities, lepers, the poor, Roman soldiers, and foreigners), and doubters (the disciples of John the Baptist and the disciple Thomas). The first four lines of each stanza describe Jesus' call to these people, and the last four lines involve us in their response.

Tune: John D. Horman wrote BLACK MOUNTAIN at the Montreat Presbyterian Music and Worship Conference in 1997, and named it after the quaint North Carolina town nearest the Montreat Conference Center. Since the text had a joyful musical motif, he set it to a light dancelike tune. The result is a hymn that is not only appropriate for congregational worship, but also for vacation Bible school or other less formal worship occasions.

Preparation

- Learn the tune, words, and movement to the song "Come, Follow Me" (See pages 78-79.)
- Make a word chart of the song and place it where all can see it.
- Practice signing the hymn or ask a helper to learn the signs to teach the children.
- Make copies of the hymn.
- Gather the art supplies.

The Session

1. Following the Leader. Use the song "Come, Follow Me" to introduce the concept of following a leader. Make sure you know the song well enough to sing each phrase for the children to imitate. Have the word chart set up where everyone (including you) can see it. Consider enlarging the music on page 78 to use as a word chart. Since the phrases are easy and the children simply echo each one in turn, you can add the movement right away.

Have the children stand in a single line, with arms outstretched and hands held loosely. Their hands must be touching, but not locked together, to allow them to move around each other in all directions. Emphasize the importance of moving carefully to avoid injuries. Ask the children to trust you and follow you as you lead them in the dance.

> *Come, follow, follow, follow me.*
> Wave your right hand and beckon the children to follow.
>
> *(Come, follow, follow, follow me.)*
> Lead the line of children and "snake" through the room.
>
> *Follow me anywhere that I lead.*
> Continue leading the line.
>
> *(Follow me anywhere that I lead.)*
> Continue leading the line.

As you finish the song, end the dance by weaving in and out of the line of dancers, starting with the child behind you and moving under the raised arms of the dancers until you have "pulled" the line completely through its own length. In some dance instructions this is called "threading the needle."

At another time, you may want to use this song as a three- or four-part canon, omitting the echoes, with a piano or Orff-style accompaniment. (See pages 80-82 for these arrangements.) *(Seven minutes)*

2. Thinking About the Dance and the Bible Story. Help the children reflect on the dance. Ask: "Who was the most important person in that dance?" If they mention the leader, point out that the followers were just as important. If any one of them had decided not to follow or tried to be the leader, the line would have been broken. People might have been hurt if someone had decided to go too fast or take a shortcut. Everyone who trusted and followed the leader was important.

Open the Bible and have one of the older children read Matthew 4:18-22. Go through the story again with the children: "Who did Jesus call? What did they do for a living? Do you think that would have been considered an important job? Were these men highly respected?" *(Point out that fishermen smelled, and they probably didn't have much money, especially when they weren't catching any fish.)*

"Do you think fishermen were leaders or followers?" Have the children explain their answers. Ask: "How do you think the fishermen felt when Jesus asked them to drop their nets and 'immediately' follow him to become 'fishers for people'? Do you think they understood what Jesus meant? Maybe, maybe not. But they still trusted him enough to follow him. He must have been very special." *(Thirteen minutes)*

3. Learning the Hymn. Pass out copies of "Jesus Sang to Fishermen." Teach this hymn in the same way as earlier hymns, with the children echo-singing the phrases one at a time after you have sung them. You can add movement by using American sign language with specific words in the text. Below is the first stanza to the hymn with signing suggestions.* *(Twenty minutes)*

Jesus sang to fishermen	**SING** Extend the left arm; pointing the fingertips of the right hand to the left palm, wave the right arm back and forth.
near the Galilee,	**SEA** Sign "water" and then "sea." (1) Form a "W" with the right hand (middle three fingers extended with thumb and little finger together), and strike the side of the mouth with the index finger several times. (2) Place the left hand behind the right palms down. Move hands up and down to indicate waves.
"Put away your nets and come,	**PUT/MOVE** Place open hands in front palms down; lift them slightly, changing to a closed position (fingertips squeezed together) as you pretend to move something to the right and set it down.
come	**COME** Index fingers rotating around each other move toward the body. Or, use the open hand in a beckoning motion.
and follow me."	**FOLLOW** Place the right "A" (fingers folded down in a straight fingered fist with thumb in vertical position) behind the left "A" and move them forward.
Jesus, sing your song to us	**SING** (See above.)
in our life today	**LIFE** Place five open fingers on both hands, palms facing the body, near the waist and draw the hands up, wiggling the fingers slightly.
We will also follow you	**FOLLOW** (See above.)
Sing to us, sing to us, sing to us,	**SING** (See above.)
we pray.	**PRAY** Place the hands palm to palm and draw them toward the body as the head is bowed slightly.

* Illustrations for the signing can be found in Lottie L. Riekehof, *Joy of Signing* (Springfield, Mo.: Gospel Publishing House, 1987).

4. Taking Turns at Leading and Following.
Move to the art center. Give each child a plain
sheet of drawing paper and place the felt-tip
pens within the children's reach. Ask them to
put their names on the back of their papers and
draw a simple shape somewhere on the front
side. Let them color their shape, using only one
colored marker. After twenty to thirty seconds,
ask the children to pass their papers to their
right and choose a different colored marker to
add a new shape to the drawing they have been
given. Encourage them to create new shapes
with each drawing. Tell them that the shapes
may touch, but they may not color over another
shape. Continue to pass the drawings in this way
until the children have their original pictures.
Ask the children to hold up their drawings, one
by one, so everyone can guess what they look
like. Then let them use glitter paints to add a

few lines, legs, arms, eyes, or other touches to
finish their drawings.

When the drawings are done, ask: "How did
you feel when you had to let other people draw
on your picture? Did you wish you could tell
them what to do next?" Comment: "We all like
to be in charge of things, but sometimes leaders
have to follow too. Look at the wonderful pieces
of art we created when we trusted that other
people had ideas to add to our drawings!"
(Fifteen minutes)

5. Praying in a Circle. Summarize the session something like this: "The disciples of Jesus
were ordinary people just like us, but they
were all important to him. They helped him in
different ways with his preaching, teaching,
and healing, and carried on his work when he
was gone. Many became leaders of the early
church, but they never forgot that they were
followers of Jesus first and must be faithful to
him. They had to work together and respect
one another's special gifts."

Ask the children to stand in a circle holding hands. Explain: "We're going to pray
together now. I'll start, and when I have finished I'll gently squeeze the hand of *(name child)*
on my left, and he/she can add a prayer
thought. We'll go all around the circle that way,
and then I'll finish." Pray this prayer or create
your own: "God, we are grateful for this time
together and for what we have learned about
following Jesus. Thank you for all the children
here and the special gifts they have to share."

When the children have all had a chance to
pray, finish the prayer: "We know that Jesus calls
us to be both leaders and followers as we carry
on his work. Help us to trust him enough to
answer his call. Amen." *(Five minutes)*

Questions for Reflection

- How did the dance serve as an introduc-
  tion to the concept of following a leader?
- Did the signing help or hinder learning
  the hymn? Why?
- How did the children respond to the
  group drawing? Did the exercise help
  them respect one another's gifts?
- How can you encourage children to take
  turns being leaders in the classroom?

Who Is Jesus?
Our Finest Friend

Something Old: "What a Friend We Have in Jesus"

Purpose: To help children discover that Jesus offers us a different kind of friendship than we are able to experience with our own friends.

Objectives: By the end of the session the children may be able to:
1. Sing the hymn, "What a Friend We Have in Jesus."
2. Name four people in the Bible whom Jesus befriended.
3. List three things that Jesus did for his friends.

Materials Needed
- Bibles, each marked with one of the references for today
- Copies of scripture commentaries for Bible study leaders
- Copies of the hymn (page 83)
- Chart board
- Four to six nonpitched percussion instruments
- Wooden matchsticks with the red end removed (three for each child)
- Plastic drop cloth
- Large container of white sculpting clay
- Markers
- Small paintbrushes
- White glue
- One piece of thin, colored yarn, cut in eighteen-inch lengths
- Fine-point tubes of puffy and slick paint in a variety of colors

Background for the Leader

Scripture: Luke 19:1-10; Luke 10:38-42; Matthew 16:13-18*a*; John 20: 24-29

The biblical references for this session are all stories about Jesus' relationships with his friends.

Luke 19:1-10

Zacchaeus, the chief tax collector in Jericho, was hated by his neighbors for his connection with the Romans who dominated their lives. Zacchaeus was a Jew like them, yet he collected revenues from them for the Roman rulers. Zacchaeus was like the most unpopular child in the classroom, the one that always does the wrong thing. When Jesus spoke to him and even went into his home for a meal, everyone was

shocked, even Zacchaeus. Hospitality was important to the Jews, and Jesus showed that God's hospitality extends to everyone, especially to sinners. Zacchaeus was so overwhelmed with joy at Jesus' generosity that he vowed to be honest in the future and pay back anyone he had defrauded. Salvation came in both Jesus' message and in Zacchaeus' response.

Luke 10:38-42

Mary and Martha and their brother Lazarus were friends of Jesus. On this occasion, Martha was so excited about having Jesus as a guest that she rushed around, wearing herself out in her determination to have the house looking nice and good food prepared to eat. She simply wanted to be hospitable, as we all do when good friends come to visit. In Bible times, women were responsible for the meal, but instead of helping her, Martha's sister Mary went to sit at Jesus' feet and talk with him. Martha, beside herself with so many tasks, complained to Jesus that Mary was not doing her share. Jesus chided her for letting her concerns distract her from the purpose of his visit, and said that Mary had chosen the better way. Jesus is honest with his friends. *(More about Jesus' relationship with this family can be found in John 8:1-44.)*

Matthew 16:13-18a

When Jesus asked his disciples what people thought of him, they reported the rumors they had heard. Then Jesus asked them what they thought. He expected a straight answer. After all, the disciples were his friends, and friends are honest and open with one another. Loyal, impetuous Peter did not disappoint him. In affirming Jesus as the Messiah, he showed evidence of the God-given faith that would become the foundation of the church. Jesus recognized that quality in him, and rejoiced.

John 20:24-29

Thomas was one of the twelve disciples who were with Jesus throughout his ministry. He was a cautious man, reluctant to believe anything that he had not witnessed himself, and he had not been there when the risen Christ had appeared. The story the disciples told was more than he could handle. Thomas needed proof, and Jesus provided that when he appeared again. Jesus understood Thomas, and loved him with all his failings, yet he made it clear that it was better to believe on the basis of faith than to ask for proof.

Hymn: "What a Friend We Have in Jesus" (CONVERSE)

Text: Life was not easy for Joseph Scriven (1819–1886), the author of "What a Friend We Have in Jesus." Poor health forced him to give up preparation for an army career. He lost two fiancées to death before they could be married. He was an Irish immigrant in Ontario, Canada, when his mother fell seriously ill in Dublin. It was out of these experiences that Scriven wrote of the friend who had never abandoned him and could always be reached through prayer. He finished the hymn in 1855, and sent it to comfort his sick mother in Ireland, never intending it to have any other use. Little did he know that it would become beloved by Christians throughout the world. The hymn was included in Horace Hastings's *Social Hymns, Original and Selected* (1865), and in Sankey's *Gospel Hymns Number One* (1875).

Another interesting fact about Scriven was his association with the Plymouth Brethren, a group of Christians who tried to live according to the Sermon on the Mount. Scriven shared everything he had with the poor and physically disabled, and as a result, was forced to live with friends because he couldn't afford a home of his own. He suffered from depression and died by drowning, either by accident or by his own hand.

Tune: Charles Crozat Converse (1832–1918) composed this tune in 1868 and named it after himself. It was included in *Silver Wings* in 1870. The composer, who practiced law in Erie, Pennsylvania for a living, wrote many hymn tunes and larger musical works, but is best remembered for this simple, easy-to-learn tune for Scriven's text.

Preparation

- Make a copy of the rhythm score for the hymn (see page 84), and give it to the adult volunteer who will be working with the percussion instruments.
- Chart the first stanza of the hymn and display it where all can see it.

- Invite three or four adult or teen assistants to be in charge of the small group Bible study. Give each leader a copy of their scripture passage and commentary.
- Gather art supplies.
- Cover the art table with a plastic cloth.

The Session

1. Discussing What Makes a Friend Special. As the children arrive engage them in conversation about friendship, using questions such as: "Why are friends important to us? What are good friends like? What makes them so special to us?" As they identify traits of friendship, record them on the chart board. Bear in mind that there may be children in the group who, at the moment, at least, feel they are without friends. Avoid putting them on the spot with personal questions like "Do you have a best friend?" *(Five minutes)*

2. Exploring Bible Stories in Small Groups. Introduce this activity something like this: "Today we're going to look at some Bible stories about Jesus and his friends, Zacchaeus, Mary and Martha, Peter, and Thomas. You will work in four groups, and each group will listen to the story and talk about it, and then act it out for the other groups. You may choose a narrator and pantomime the story, or assign different people to read the speaking parts in the story, or you can make up your own words for the characters."

Divide the children into four groups, each with an adult or teen assistant. These group leaders should familiarize themselves with the assigned scripture and commentary ahead of time, so they are prepared to read the story and help the group reflect on it, and be ready to suggest some options for dramatizing the story if the children need help in planning. For example:

Group 1: Jesus and Zacchaeus (Luke 19:1-10). Jesus was a friend to people who had no other friends. Additional characters could be onlookers in the crowd.

Group 2: Jesus and Mary and Martha (Luke 10:38-42). Jesus helps his friends see what is really important in life. Props could include some cooking pots and baskets.

Group 3: Jesus and Peter (Matthew 16:13-18a). Jesus was interested in his friends' thoughts and opinions, not just his own. He recognized that God had gifted Peter with faith, saw the potential he had for being a leader of the church, and encouraged him in that direction. The other disciples who were with Jesus and Peter in Caesarea Philippi could also be in the story.

Group 4: Jesus and Thomas (John 20:24-29). Jesus accepted Thomas with all his doubts and satisfied his need for proof, but also challenged him with the higher goal of believing on faith. Some of the children could play the other disciples.

Allow eight minutes for the planning process, and three minutes for each skit. When all the skits have been shared, ask the children to help make a list of why the disciples might have considered Jesus their "finest friend." *(For example: Jesus was kind to everyone, made people want to become better persons, wanted to hear his friends' ideas, appreciated and encouraged their special gifts, accepted their faults but challenged them to improve.)* Record their responses on a chart to use later in the worship time. Then ask: "How was the way Jesus treated his friends different from the way we treat our friends?" Allow time for the children to respond. Conclude with this comment: "Maybe we all need to learn from Jesus how to be better friends to one another." *(Twenty minutes)*

3. Making Friendship Beads. Have the children move to the art table that you have covered with the plastic drop cloth. Give each child a lump of clay, enough for them to shape into three large marble-sized beads. Show the children how to pull the clay into three pieces and roll the clay between the palms of their hands to round each bead. When the beads are made, use the matchstick to poke a hole through the middle of each bead. Leave the bead on the matchstick until it is painted. Give each child another lump of clay (or polystyrene foam, florist oasis, or an

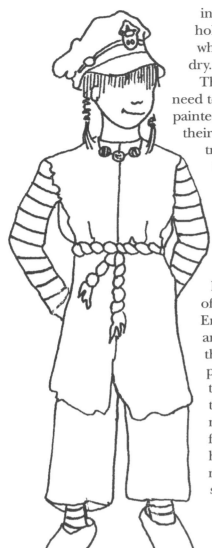

inverted paper cup) to hold the matchsticks while the painted beads dry.

The clay beads do not need to dry before they are painted, but they will lose their shape if they are treated roughly. Caution the children to handle them carefully. Have them use small paintbrushes to decorate their beads, or paint applied directly from the fine point of the paint tubes. Encourage them to use any patterns or designs they like. When the paint is dry, tell them to push the matchstick through the bead, moving it back and forth to make sure the hole is clean, and then remove the matchstick. *(Fifteen minutes)*

4. Learning the Hymn. Display the word chart for "What a Friend We Have in Jesus" so that it can be seen from anywhere in the room. Introduce the hymn something like this: "The man who wrote this hymn had many troubles in his life that made him feel very much alone, except for his 'finest friend' who was always there for him." Explain that you are going to sing the first stanza of the hymn while they listen. Ask them to raise their hands when they hear long pitches in the melody. Have a helper underline the words that fall on those pitches in the text on the chart.

Tell the children that the hymn makes a fine march, especially when percussion instruments are added. Have ready four to six rhythm instruments for selected children to play, and let them form a small percussion ensemble to accompany the hymn, with the percussion rhythm score on page 84 as a guide. Try to avoid using more than a third of the children as instrumentalists. Ask another adult to be in charge of the percussion ensemble and help them find the steady beat, the accented beat, and the rhythm of the words.

Instruct the remaining children to sing along with the hymn while they march in different directions, respecting the people and objects in the room. Explain that on each long pitch in the hymn, they are to stop and shake hands with the person closest to them. Tell them there will be no time for conversations; when the music moves on from the long pitch, so must they. Let them repeat the process as time allows, with different people playing the percussion instruments each time. *(Fifteen minutes)*

5. Share Some Beads and a Prayer. Have the children get the beads they made and come sit in a circle near the chart board. Give them each a piece of colored yarn to thread through their beads to make a friendship necklace, but tell them that before they string their beads, they must give two of them away, one to the child on their left and one to the child on their right. Once this has been accomplished, let the children string the beads and tie the ends of the yarn together for a necklace. As they work, ask them: "How did you decide which beads to give away and which to keep?" *(Some may have kept the best for themselves, while others may have given away their favorites. Pick up on the latter.)* Comment: "Friends are very special when they give us something precious to them. Jesus was that kind of 'finest friend.' He spent his life sharing God's love with us."

Quickly review the list of ways Jesus acted toward his friends. Then line out this prayer, phrase by phrase, for the children to echo: "Thank you, God, for Jesus, our 'finest friend.' Help us follow his example in our friendships with one another. Amen." *(Five minutes)*

Questions for Reflection————

After the children have left, consider the session:

- How did the addition of percussion instruments motivate children who are not as interested in singing?
- What did the children learn about being a good friend from the Bible stories? Did they enjoy doing the skits?
- How did the art project help the children expand their idea of friendship?

5-B Who Is Jesus?
Our Finest Friend

*Something New: "Emmanuel,
Who Walked Among Us Here"*

Purpose: To help children discover that they can learn how to be better
friends to one another by following the example of Jesus and listening to his words.

Objectives: By the end of the session the children may be able to:
1. Explain why friendships are different from other kinds of relationships.
2. Tell what the disciples learned from Jesus about friendship.
3. Sing the refrain of the hymn.
4. Contribute to a project that involves an act of friendship for someone
   beyond their own peer group.

Materials Needed
- Bible
- Copies of the hymn (page 85)
- Piano or keyboard
- Chart board
- Markers
- White glue
- Eight-inch squares of prewashed white cot-
  ton broadcloth (one for each child)
- Eight-inch squares of prewashed pastel
  cotton broadcloth (enough to create an
  even number of total squares)

- Die-cut sponges in shapes such as butter-
  flies, birds, animals, angels, flowers, stars,
  and hearts, or similar designs cut from
  compressed sponge sheets (available in
  most art or craft supply stores or catalogs)
- Tubes of permanent "block printing
  glazes" in a variety of soft, cheerful colors
- Small saucers for holding glaze
- Quilt batting
- Soft material for quilt backing
- Yarn and large yarn needle
- Plastic drop cloth to protect the table
- Sheet for laying out the squares

Background for the Leader

Scripture: John 15:12-15

This scripture is part of the chapter in the
Gospel of John that describes three dimen-
sions of the Christian life: the believers' relationship to Christ (John 15:1-11); to one
another (John 15:12-17); and to the world
(John 15:18-27). The second section inspired
this hymn. In this passage, Jesus commands his
disciples to love one another in the same way
that he has loved them. Hinting at what lay

ahead, he tells them that laying down one's
life for one's friends is the greatest love of all.
He continues by explaining that a friend is different from a slave or a servant who follows
orders without question. Friends share all that
they know of God's love, as Jesus has shared
with them. He expects them to follow the way
of love they have learned and experienced
through their friendship.

Hymn: "Emmanuel, Who Walked Among Us Here" (KENSINGTON)

Text: Hymn texts sometimes go through several revisions before they reach their final form. Mary Nelson Keithahn wrote the first version of this hymn to help Christians affirm and express a living faith in times of crisis, and dedicated it to the memory of those lost to AIDS. After a sermon she heard on John 15:12-17 started her thinking about Jesus' definition of his followers as "friends," she revised her text to focus on Jesus as our "finest friend" and emphasize Jesus' concept of friendship as the basis for the covenantal relationships that are so important in the life of God's people. Each stanza addresses one aspect of those relationships, noting both the role of Jesus and our call to carry on his work.

Tune: John D. Horman named his tune KENSINGTON after Kensington, Maryland, the site of Warner Memorial Presbyterian Church, where he has served as director of music since 1970. The sense of walking forward in the tune's refrain symbolizes both the way that Jesus traveled in his ministry and our personal progression through lives of faith.

Preparation

- Make copies of the hymn.
- Purchase materials for the quilt (white and pastel fabric for the eight-inch squares, fabric for back, and batting) in quantities needed for the number of children in your group.
- Gather the other art supplies.
- Recruit one or more persons from your congregation to sew the children's squares together, add the batting and backing, and either tie the quilt or machine quilt it.
- Select and contact a charity or hospital that will accept a small quilt as a gift for a sick baby.

The Session

1. Discussing Key Words. Write these words on the chalkboard or a chart board: *Leader, Follower (Servant), Friends.* Ask: "How are these words different in meaning?" Accept their replies, and then add to your list as follows:
Leader—Walks ahead.
Follower (Servant)—Walks behind.
Friends—Sometime one leads and the other follows, but often walk side by side.

Invite the children's comments on what you have written. *(Three to five minutes)*

2. Learning the Hymn. Pass out copies of "Emmanuel, Who Walked Among Us Here." Explain: "Today we're going to work with a hymn about friends. There are five stanzas, and each one is about Jesus, our 'finest friend.' Notice that one line in each stanza is the same. What do we call the part of a hymn that is repeated in each stanza? (Refrain.) Find it on your copy. This is the part of the hymn that we are going to learn. It will be used as a prayer response in our last session."

Sing "May we walk, may we walk" and ask the children to echo-sing. Ask: "In what direction are we going, up or down?" (Down.) Finish singing the phrase (last word "end"). Ask: "Where did we go next?" (Continued down and then soared up.) Have everyone sing the phrase with you while following the music with their index finger. Then sing the second phrase and ask the children to listen. Sing it again and ask the children to trace the melody line in the air as they echo-sing. Generally, what direction does this phrase move? (Down.) Sing the whole refrain now with the children tracing its contour in the air as you sing.

Here is a way to add simple but effective choreography to the refrain: The children stand in a circle, turn to the right, and moving counterclockwise, follow the person in front of them around the circle on "May we walk, may we walk" (four steps). Then on "with each other till life's end" they reverse direction and walk, still single file, to the left (four steps). On "not as servant, nor a slave" they turn to face into the circle, join hands, and walk three steps to the center with hands raised. On "but as a friend" they drop one neighbor's hand but keep the other and walk three steps back to the circle, bowing respectfully to their partners when they reach their place. (Note: If there is an uneven number of children in the group, you or another leader should take part in the dance so everyone will have a partner.)

Sing the first two stanzas of the song alone, encouraging the children to dance and sing the refrain each time it occurs. Then ask: "How does the dance help us understand the difference between how people act as slaves and servants and as friends?" *(Twenty minutes)*

3. Thinking About Jesus' Words. Introduce John 15:12-15 something like this: "The disciples of Jesus call him Master, but he never treats them as slaves or even servants. He considers them his friends. Even though he is the leader and they are his followers, they have walked together carrying the good news of God's love throughout the land. Three years have passed, and Jesus knows that the end of his earthly ministry is near. He wants to share everything God has told him with his friends. What does Jesus say to them?"

Read the scripture and then comment: "Jesus

said that the greatest love of all was giving your life for your friends. What do you think about that idea? Have you heard of people who lost their lives trying to save their friends? *(Allow time for responses.)* How would you feel about someone who stepped in front of a car to push you out of harm's way, or shielded you from falling rock in an earthquake or rescued you in a fire? How could you thank them enough for that kind of friendship?"

Comment: "After Jesus died, his friends probably wondered how they could possibly thank God enough for all their friend had meant to them. Perhaps they remembered Jesus' words: 'Love one another, as I have loved you.' Perhaps that's why they gave their lives to the work of the church." *(Ten to twelve minutes)*

4. Making a Friendship Quilt. Explain: "Today we're going to print designs on squares of cloth. A member of the church will sew the squares together later into a friendship quilt to keep a sick child comfortable and warm." Show the children the glazes and sponges you have laid out on the table. *(Make sure you have a variety so the children will have a*

Directions for Sewing the Quilt

With painted sides facing, pin together two squares and sew along one side, using a 1/4-inch seam. (The seams need to be accurate or the rows will not match.) Continue adding squares in this way until the first row is assembled. Then do the other rows. When all the rows are completed, press each one. Iron all the seams in the row in one direction, reverse the direction in the second row, and continue alternating in that manner on remaining rows. (This will facilitate butting the seams together.) Pin the rows together with painted sides facing and seams matching, and sew all rows together, again using a 1/4-inch seam, to form the quilt top. (See diagram.)

Cut the batting and backing an inch larger

than the size of the quilt top to ensure having enough of each when the layers are sandwiched together. (The excess can be trimmed after the quilt is sewn together.) Baste the backing to the quilt top around the outside edges. With right sides facing, pin the quilt backing to the quilt top and baste together. Machine stitch a seam around the quilt, leaving a ten- to twelve-inch opening on one side. Trim the seams, and turn the quilt so the right sides are outside and the batting is inside. Hand stitch the opening together, tucking the raw edges inside. Tie the quilt with yarn at the corners of each square to hold the layers in place. Wash the quilt on gentle cycle with gentle detergent before presentation.

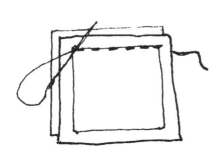 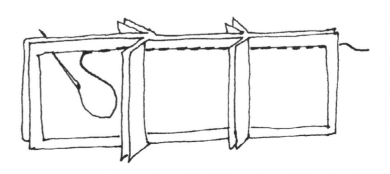

choice.) On a sample piece of cloth, demonstrate how to press a sponge first into the glaze and then carefully onto the square. Stress the importance of lifting the sponge straight up and off of the cloth so it does not smear. Remind the children to wash each sponge after they have used it, so that others may use it too. (*If you do not have access to a sink, have a large dishpan of soapy water and paper towels available.*) Let the children print four or five designs in different colors on their squares, and then set them aside carefully to dry. When the cloth is dry, help them sign their names on their squares with a light-colored, fine-tip, permanent marker, making sure that the letters are small and do not overpower the designs. Let the children help arrange the squares onto a sheet in a square or slightly rectangular shape like a blanket. If you end up with an odd number of painted squares, use plain squares of pastel cotton to fill in and balance your design. Assure the children that once the squares are assembled and quilted, they will get to see the finished quilt before it is given away. (*Twenty minutes*)

Note: Try to have the quilt done in time to display at the closing hymn sing service.

5. Praying Together.
Bring or borrow a handmade quilt to use in your worship time. Spread it out on the floor and ask the children to sit around the edges. Comment: "Someone must have worked very hard to make this beautiful quilt. Do you suppose it was a gift for a friend or someone else they loved?" If you know the story of the quilt, take a few minutes to share it with the children. Then walk over and look again at their quilt squares. Comment: "We know how hard you worked to decorate your squares for the quilt we're going to give to (*name the recipient of your quilt*) after it is finished. The (*child*) will feel your love in the warmth of the quilt and know you are (*his/her*) friends."

Invite the children to pray with you as you line out this prayer for them to echo: "God, we thank you for Jesus, our finest friend, who showed us how to be a friend to others. May the child who receives our quilt look upon it as a gift of love from friends who are trying to follow the way of Jesus. Amen." (*Five minutes*)

Questions for Reflection——————
- How did the dance movements to the hymn help the children differentiate between servant, slave, and friend?
- How did the discussion of the passage from John prepare the children for the quilt project?
- What are some other ways that children can befriend persons outside their peer group?

Who Is Jesus?
Our Teacher

Something Old: "It's Me, It's Me, O Lord"

Purpose: To help children explore a teaching of Jesus about the blessings received by the "poor in spirit" and relate that idea to our need for prayer.

Objectives: By the end of the session the children may be able to:
1. Share times in their lives when they have felt blessed.
2. Talk about the blessing that comes from trusting God in difficult times.
3. Sing the spiritual, "It's Me, It's Me, O Lord," and feel comfortable singing certain lines alone.
4. Compare the hymn with a psalm and a Beatitude.

Materials Needed
- Bible
- Copies of the hymn (page 87)
- Piano or keyboard
- Chart board
- Markers, including a light green marker and three dark green fine-line markers
- Ladder chart from Session 3-A
- Mat board, 12" x 36" (vary the length according to number of children) in white, cream, pale blue, or pale yellow
- Washable ink pads in bright colors
- Access to sink or pan of soapy water and paper towels for cleanup

Background for the Leader

Scripture: Psalm 3:1-6; Matthew 5:2-12

Both scriptures affirm that for those who trust in God, the difficult times of life can be a blessing because it is in then that we are most aware of our dependence on God, our need to pray for guidance, and our joy in God's presence.

Psalm 3:1-6

Like the African American spirituals that long for God to free them from bondage, this psalm asks for deliverance from personal enemies. Although these "songs of deliverance" lament difficult personal situations, they are also expressions of trust in God, affirming that God is present and active in the world, no matter how bad things look.

Matthew 5:2-12

The Beatitudes are part of the Sermon on the Mount, a collection of Jesus' teachings that were the basis of the new age he had come to introduce. Speaking from the seated position of a Jewish rabbi to emphasize the importance of his words, Jesus answered the people's psalms of lament with a message of hope. People who try hard to let God rule their lives receive special blessings.

Hymn: "It's Me, It's Me, O Lord" (PENITENT)

Text: The origin of this African American spiritual, like many folk songs, is unknown. It became popular after it was published in *The*

Book of American Negro Spirituals (1925), compiled by James Weldon Johnson and his brother, J. Rosamond Johnson. The hymn expresses the longings of slaves who knew they had no one but God to call upon for their deliverance from bondage. Although the individual's need to communicate with God in prayer is stressed, the fact that other persons are mentioned indicates that this is a need shared by others in the same situation. Everyone who has sinned is "standing in the need of prayer."

Tune: In most songbooks and hymnals, this spiritual is harmonized in a major key and sung lightly at a moderate tempo. However, if workers had sung the song outdoors in the field, with one group singing a phrase and another group answering ("call and response"), it might have sounded quite different. Perhaps the tempo would have slowed down to match the hard work the slaves were doing. As the singing spread from one individual to another across the fields, overlapping harmonies would have been created, resulting in a minor mode and heavier mood. It would be interesting to try singing the spiritual in this way and experience the different effect.

Preparation

- Make copies of the hymn.
- Enlarge the Pitch Continuum Chart for the display board (see page 53).
- Gather the art supplies.
- Prepare the banner for the art project. (Indicate that the long side is the bottom by using a light green marker to draw the suggestion of grass. The children will add to this later.)
- Optional: Make a copy of the Prayer Ladder (Session 3-A) as a visual aid in singing the hymn.

The Session

1. Sharing Stories. As the children gather, say : "I felt especially blessed this week. So many good things happened to me." Go on to share a few experiences, and then ask: "When was a time that you felt especially blessed? What happened to make you feel that way?" Encourage the children to share their stories, and summarize each one in a short sentence on the chart board. *(Five minutes)*

2. Creating a "Fingerprint Flower Garden." Move to the art table. Post the list of sentences you have recorded where everyone can see it. Explain: "We're going to make a banner today showing some of the ways God blesses us as we grow. Find the sentence on the chart that tells about your blessing. Use a green fine-line marker to write your sentence on the mat board so it will look like the stem of a flower growing out of the grass across the bottom of the board." *(If your group is large, use several mat boards and ask other leaders to help.)*

When the children have completed their "stems," show them how to make the flowers. First, have them press their thumbs on a colored ink pad and make a thumbprint at the top of their stems. Then show them how to press their other four fingers on the ink pads to print the flower petals. (See page 53.) Let them wash the ink off their hands in the sink or a pan of soapy water. After they finish, let them use light green markers to add more grass along the bottom of the board, taking care not to cover up their flower stems. At the top of the drawing use colored markers to print, "It's me, it's me, O Lord . . . Growing in the Garden of God." Ask the children what makes each flower unique (the thumbprints) and comment: "Isn't it wonderful that God loves each one of us, and blesses us with what we need to grow!" *(Fifteen minutes)*

Note: If you plan to use the hymn sing at the end of the course, keep this banner in a safe place to display then.

3. Singing the Hymn. Like their fingerprints, the voice of each child is unique, a product of genetics and vocal experience. Probably no two voices in your group are in the same place developmentally. In order to help the

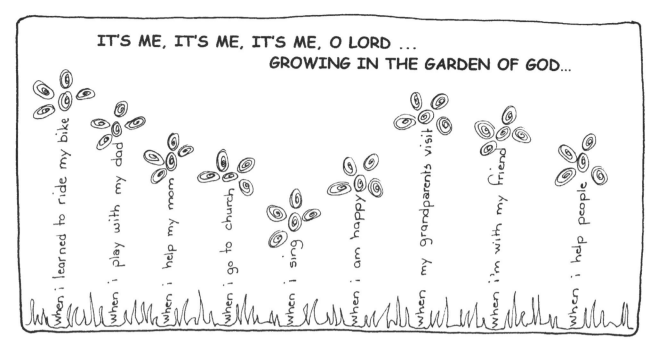

IT'S ME, IT'S ME, IT'S ME, O LORD ...
GROWING IN THE GARDEN OF GOD...

when i learned to ride my bike
when i play with my dad
when i help my mom
when i go to church
when i sing
when i am happy
when my grandparents visit
when i'm with my friend
when i help people

children grow vocally in areas that need improvement, you will need to listen to them individually. "It's Me, It's Me, O Lord" can be used to help children gain confidence in matching pitch and singing both alone and in front of their peers. Keep in mind that most children can grow and mature as singers in a nonjudgmental, nurturing environment. You can establish that climate of trust in your group by being supportive of each singer's efforts, correcting vocal problems gently, and encouraging accuracy and good tonal quality in every voice.

Gather the children around the piano. Introduce "It's Me, It's Me, O Lord," as a hymn African Americans sang when they were working long, hard hours out in the fields. They counted few blessings in their lives, and they looked to God for help. This hymn is about their need to pray.

Give photocopies of the hymn to the children. Explain: "In order to sing this hymn well, we need to be able to match pitch." Note that two things are important: (1) where the sound is placed on a continuum from low to high (refer to Pitch Continuum Chart); and (2) the intervals or relationships between pitches.

Write on the display board: "Listen . . . think . . . and then sing!" and tell the children this is what good singing requires. Have them repeat the words together.

Sing the first "It's me" from the refrain of the hymn, and ask the children to echo-sing it—first all together, next in small groups, then a few at a time, and finally one by one. Sing the second "It's me" for the children to imitate, and ask: "Are the two phrases the same or different?" (They are the same.) Now sing, "It's me, O Lord!" for the children to echo. Ask: "How is this phrase different from the first two we sang?" (It moves down by step.)

Line out the refrain, one phrase at a time, for the children to echo-sing. Then ask the children: "What happens to the melody for 'Standing in the need of prayer' the second time it is sung?" If they have not noticed the dif-

PITCH CONTINUUM

VERY HIGH!!!!
HIGH!
A LITTLE HIGH
MEDIUM
A LITTLE LOW
LOW
VERY LOW

ferent endings, sing the lines again for them to echo. Use the Prayer Ladder (see Session 3-A) to explain that "Standing" is sung on Rung #1, and ask someone to show how the different endings move up or down the ladder. (The first progression is 1-1-1-1-2-2-3 and the second is 1-1-1-1-3-2-1.)

Explain: "We need three children to sing the short phrases in the first line alone, one for 'It's me,' one for the second 'it's me,' and another for 'it's me, O Lord.' They will sing that line each time while the rest of us sing 'Standing in the need of prayer.' Who would like to volunteer?" (Some should feel comfortable enough with the hymn by now to offer. If you have too many volunteers, tell them they can take turns and sing the parts on alternate stanzas.)

Now sing all the stanzas of the hymn, with the children singing the refrain as above. If there is time and the children are enjoying the hymn, encourage them to make up additional stanzas, noting that this is probably how people began singing this hymn. (Twenty minutes)

4. Comparing the Hymn, a Psalm, and a Beatitude. Read Psalm 3:1-6. Ask: "How is this psalm like the hymn we just sang?" Point out that these songs both came from people who were feeling tired, troubled, hopeless, and in need of God's help. They sang to remind themselves that the God they trusted was always with them and would hear their prayers.

Open your Bible to Matthew 5:1-3, and comment: "This is the beginning of a section in the Gospel of Matthew called the Sermon on the Mount. The sermon is a collection of Jesus' teachings, and it includes a group of nine sayings known as the Beatitudes. Each Beatitude begins with the word *Blessed.* What do you think that word means?" (Allow time for the children to respond, then continue.) "When we counted our blessings, we remembered times when we were happy, when good things happened to us, when we felt especially loved. But Jesus said, 'Blessed are the poor in spirit.' The 'poor in spirit' sound like people who are in as much trouble as the ones who were singing the psalm and the hymn! Why would they feel blessed?"

Explain to the children that the words of Jesus help us understand that being "poor in spirit" is really a blessing. When we realize we have no power to change the way things are, we can only trust in God to help us. Trusting God makes us willing to follow God's way of love, and that is what brings us true joy and happiness, even when life goes wrong for us. This was the experience of the Hebrews long ago, and the African Americans working in the fields. It is still true today. (Ten minutes)

If there is time you might continue the discussion by asking: "Can you think of anyone you know who found that a disappointment or unhappy situation turned out to be a blessing when they took it to God in prayer?" Be ready with some examples to share. For example:

- A talented child loses a much-desired part in a play because he has not prepared for the audition, but he works hard to prepare for the next audition, asks God to help him do his best, and gets a part.
- A basketball player, confined to a wheelchair after a car accident, asks God to help her find something else to fill her time, and finds new joy in tutoring younger children in need of help.

Conclude: "We can find unexpected blessings in discouraging situations when we trust in God enough to ask God's help in prayer."

5. Ending with a Prayer. Display your new banner. Let children who want to share their blessing "stems" read their sentences aloud.

Then offer a prayer something like this: "Dear God, we are grateful to you for blessing us with people who love us and everything we need to live, but most of all we thank you for Jesus who taught us that being 'poor in spirit' was a blessing too. We know we cannot solve all our problems by ourselves. When we feel discouraged, hurt, or disappointed, help us trust in you and bring our needs to you in prayer, that we might find the greatest blessing of all, the joy and peace of your love. Amen. *(Five minutes)*

Questions for Reflection

- What did you learn about the children's concept of "blessing" from the stories they shared for the banner project?
- How did the teachings of Jesus help the children connect the experiences of the psalm and the hymn with discouraging times in the lives of people today?
- How can you help the children use prayer to discover God's blessings in difficult situations?

6-B Who Is Jesus? Our Teacher

Something New: "Up to the Temple One Fine Day"

Purpose: To help children experience and gain insights from a story that Jesus told about the importance of humility and honesty in prayer.

Objectives: By the end of the session the children may be able to:
1. Retell the story of the Pharisee and the tax collector in their own words.
2. Sing the hymn "Up to the Temple One Fine Day."
3. Begin to understand the concept of humility.

Materials Needed
- Bible
- Copies of the hymn (page 88)
- Piano and keyboard
- Chart board
- Biblical costumes for the dramatization
- Border template
- Gold, medium-point marker
- Precut white mat board 8½" x 11" (one for each child)
- Soft, round chalk pastels in a variety of light to medium colors
- Stencils of birds in flight (available at art and craft stores)
- Kneaded rubber erasers, one for every two children
- Unscented hair spray

Background for the Leader

Scripture: Luke 18:9-14

Jesus often used stories to teach about God. This parable compares two different men who go to the temple to pray. The first is a holy man, a Pharisee, who has dedicated his life to his religion. He knows and obeys all the laws and rituals of the Jews, including fasting on Mondays and Thursdays and giving one-tenth of his income to the temple. A proud man, he believes God loves him more than those who do not obey the law, and goes so far as to make a list of "sinners" who do not measure up. He shows no mercy to them. The second man, a sinner in the eyes of the Pharisee, does not consider himself worthy of God's love. He asks for nothing but God's mercy.

Jesus observed that the second man who came to pray was the one who was "justified," that is, accepted by God, because he showed by his prayer that he recognized his need for mercy and forgiveness. God can only help us when we pray with honesty and humility instead of building up ourselves at the expense of others.

Hymn: "Up to the Temple One Fine Day" (WHEATON)

Tune: Mary Nelson Keithahn wanted to write a hymn text on a parable that would have meaning for children as well as adults, and finally settled on the story of two men who went up to the temple to pray (Luke 18:9-14). She felt that children would relate to this story Jesus told to people who "trusted in themselves that they were righteous and regarded others with contempt," since children are quick to complain about peers who are "stuck up and know it all." The hymn is a poetic paraphrase of the parable, suggesting that, although we are all tempted to think that we are better then others, Jesus reminds us that we are all equals in God's eyes: people who make mistakes and need God's love.

Tune: John D. Horman set this text to a tune he named WHEATON after a Maryland suburb near his Silver Spring home.

Preparation

- Make copies of the hymn.
- Chart the five stanzas of the hymn.
- Ask two of the older children to take the roles of the Pharisee and tax collector. Have them read the story from the Bible ahead of time so they will be familiar with their lines and can read them with expression. Give each one a biblical costume to wear. If possible, rehearse the dramatization with them ahead of time.
- Gather the art supplies.

- Copy the border template (page 60) and cut out the design. Center the template on one of the mat boards, and trace the border with a gold marker. Repeat for each mat board.
- Purchase stencils of birds in flight from a local art store or copy pictures to make your own.
- Break all chalk pastels in half so that the children can share them more easily.

The Session

1. Talking About Bragging. As the children gather, ask: "What does the word *brag* mean?" *(Some dictionary definitions are: boast, pat oneself on the back, talk in an arrogant or pompous manner.)* "When was the last time you bragged about something to someone else? What was it about and to whom were you talking?" Accept all the responses without comment. *(Five minutes)*

2. Dramatizing and Discussing a Bible Story. Introduce the story something like this: "There are always people who want to make sure that everyone knows how important they are. Jesus had a story for some people like that. It is one of those stories from everyday life that has a lesson for us to learn about God. We call those stories *parables*. This parable is a story about two very different men. One is a Pharisee, an important leader of the synagogue. The other is a tax collector, like Zacchaeus. I've asked two children to help me tell this story."

Let the costumed "Pharisee" and "Tax Collector" take their places for the skit. Read the narrative parts of Luke 18:10-14 as children act it out and speak their lines. Then ask the others: "Which of the two men was bragging?"

(The Pharisee was a proud man, and wanted God to notice how much better he was at following the laws than ordinary people.) "What did the other man do?" *(The tax collector was a humble man. He knew who he was and how much he needed God's love.)* "According to Jesus, which man pleased God most? Why?"

Comment: "Does this mean that we can't be proud and happy about our accomplishments? Not at all. Jesus was trying to teach us that no matter how hard we try, we all fall short of being the kind of persons God meant us to be. The Pharisee was a holy man, but he built himself up by looking down on his neighbors. He forgot that all our talents and accomplishments are gifts from God to be used for helping others, and he was keeping those gifts for himself. He needed God's forgiveness just as much as the tax collector did." *(Fifteen minutes)*

3. Learning the Hymn. Use a large chart with the words for the five stanzas of "Up to the Temple One Fine Day" to teach the hymn. Explain that the hymn tells the same story as the parable in poetic form. Read all five stanzas with the children, discussing and explaining the meaning of any words that they might not recognize (*unique, fast, tithe, resume, righteous*) and how the two main characters are different in their approach to God. Then use the first stanza of the hymn to teach the melody. Sing each of the four phrases and ask the children to echo-sing them until they are secure with the stanza.

Ask the children who played the Pharisee and the tax collector in the earlier dramatization to pantomime the story as you sing it. Explain that pantomime is different from dramatization because it uses silent movement and facial expressions instead of speech to tell a story. Discuss how each character can let the audience know who they are without using words. Sing through the hymn.

Then ask: "How can we sing the words of the Pharisee and the tax collector so that we sound like the characters are acting?" (*Louder and accented for the Pharisee, softer and smoother for the tax collector.*) Sing the hymn again more expressively, with other children playing the two characters. If time is short, choose two children to read the last two stanzas of the hymn instead of singing it. (*Twenty minutes*)

4. Making a Chalk Picture. Have the children come to the art center. Give them each a

mat board with the border marked on it, and suggest that they choose three or four pieces of chalk in colors that express how they feel. Ask the children to apply the colors gently to area inside the border on the mat board, using the sides of the pastels, taking care that the colors touch, but do not cover one another. When the children have finished with this step, show them how to use their fingers to blend the colors in a circular motion. Then give each child a stencil and a kneaded rubber eraser with these instructions: "Place the bird anywhere you wish on the board, hold it down firmly, and erase the color to define the bird's natural form."

As the white birds appear on their boards, comment: "We love to look at all these beautiful colors on our boards, but underneath the colors, the boards are still white. It's the same with us. God rejoices in all our unique personalities, talents, and accomplishments, but loves us for the persons we are inside. God wants us to be those persons when we pray."

Help the children express this idea in simple sentences on their mat boards around the outside of the border (e.g., God loves me for who I really am). Be sure to have them clean up the area first with the erasers. When they have finished writing their sentences, spray each piece with unscented hair spray to fix the chalk. (*Fifteen minutes*)

5. Sharing a Prayer. Introduce the prayer something like this: "We know Jesus said we shouldn't come to prayer 'puffed up' and bragging about our achievements, but sometimes we want to share the good things we have done with God. How do you think we can do this?" Listen to their ideas and then comment: "Maybe the best way to share our accomplishments with God is through a prayer of thanksgiving, because it is God who has made them possible."

Ask the children to join hands and think of something about themselves that makes them thankful. Explain: "I will begin the prayer and then we'll go around the circle to the left so everyone can add a thought. When you have finished, or if you want to pass, squeeze the hand of the person on your left. I'll finish the prayer when we have gone around the circle." Begin something like this:

"God, we are glad that Jesus taught us that you love us as we are, and we don't have to brag about the things we have done to impress you. We are so grateful for all you have given us, and we want to thank you for. . . . *(Squeeze the hand of the child at your left. When the squeeze gets back to you, say what you are grateful for and end the prayer.)* For all these gifts and more we give you thanks and praise. Amen." *(Five minutes)*

Questions for Reflection

- Which is harder: coming to God with our achievements or with our faults?
- What did the children learn about sharing their accomplishments with God in prayer?
- Think about the things that impress our friends. Then think about the things that impress God. Are they the same?

7 Who Is Jesus? A Hymn Sing

Purpose: To help the children learn some of the different ways hymns can be used in worship, experience what it is like to lead worship, and share the hymns they have been singing with their families and others in the congregation.

Objectives: By the end of the session the children may be able to:
1. Sing at least the refrain or one stanza of all the hymns they have learned in this course.
2. Demonstrate that they are able to assist in leading worship.
3. Name at least three ways hymns can be used as elements of worship.
4. Share the hymns they have learned with their parents and other adults in their faith community.

Materials Needed

- Bible
- Copies of all the hymns that are not in your church's hymnal
- Biblical costumes for the two children that will participate in the sermon
- Scripted order of worship for the hymn sing (page 62)
- Worship bulletin for participants
- Group prayer written by the children (3-A)
- An art project from each pair of sessions: Shepherd Banner (1-B); Advocate Image (2-B); Prayer Ladder (3-A); Windsong Mobile (4-A); Friendship Quilt (5-B); Fingerprint Flower Garden Banner (6-A)

Background for the Leader

The hymn sing will provide an opportunity for the children to sing again all the hymns they have learned in this course, and to share what they have learned about Jesus with their families and others in the congregation. They will also display an art project from each pair of sessions in the worship center.

In the worship order for this hymn sing, most of the elements of worship are sung, except for a group prayer and a scripture reading by the children, a dramatized reading of the parable about the Pharisee and the tax collector, and a welcome and benediction by a pastor or teacher. However, the script provides for one or more narrators to explain each element in the service as a way of helping the children and other participants understand the different acts of worship. The narrator(s) should be adults.

On several of the hymns the children will sing a stanza or refrain alone. They should probably stand and face the congregation when they sing. Some children may also be playing in an Orff-type percussion ensemble.

Children may also serve as greeters and ushers for this service, and several could be assigned to interpret the art projects on display before the service begins.

Preparation

- Invite the pastor(s) of your church to participate in the worship service (giving the welcome and/or benediction, serving as narrator).
- Arrange for someone to accompany the hymns. If you are also going to add Orff-type accompaniments, rehearse those ahead of time.
- Duplicate the scripted order of worship for leaders, and abbreviated orders for the other participants.
- Make multiple copies of the hymns not found in your hymnal as needed.
- Arrange the art projects attractively in the worship area. Label each one with the theme it represents, and add signs naming the paired hymns for the theme.
- Ask the children who were the Pharisee and tax collector for the dramatization in Session 6-B to repeat their roles in the hymn sing. Give each one a costume to wear. Rehearse with them ahead of time, especially if the hymn sing will be in the sanctuary instead of the classroom. *(You may also want to assign an older child or a pastor or teacher to read the narrative role of Jesus in the story.)*
- Choose other children to read the first scripture lesson and the original group prayer from Session 3-A, and practice with them until they are comfortable with their assignments.
- Determine who will benefit from the offering that will be taken in the service, and choose some of the children to serve as ushers.
- Optional: Copy the Hymn Sing invitation (page 92) for the children to color and give to family and friends.
- Optional: Copy the Certificate of Participation (page 93) and fill in the information (one per child) to give to the children.

WHO IS JESUS? A HYMN SING

THE GATHERING

(As the children gather with their families and other members of the congregation, suggest that they look at the art projects in the worship area and encourage the children to interpret them. At the appointed time, ask everyone to take their places for the hymn sing. Seat the children together at the front of the congregation so they can stand to lead the singing.)

WORDS OF WELCOME

Pastor or Teacher: The children and I welcome you to this special service of worship. Over the past few months we have been getting better acquainted with Jesus by looking at some of the roles he has played in the life of the church. We have discovered Jesus as our Shepherd, Advocate, Way to God, Leader, Finest Friend, and Teacher. In our sessions, we have sung both old and new hymns, heard stories from the Bible, and created wonderful art projects, some of which you see in our worship center. Now we invite you to join us as we sing our way through the worship order and remember all that Jesus means to us today. You will notice that we have used hymns for most of the acts of worship, instead of the spoken word. A narrator will explain each act before we sing.

CALL TO WORSHIP

Narrator: The call to worship God comes to us from Jesus through words spoken and sung, reminding us to lay aside the cares and demands of everyday life and focus our attention on God. Let us all sing one stanza of "Jesus Calls Us O'er the Tumult."

Hymn: "Jesus Calls Us O'er the Tumult" (GALILEE), stanza 1

HYMN OF PRAISE

Narrator: Praise is our joyful response to the amazing gift of God in Jesus, our Good Shepherd. Let us praise God by singing "The King of Love My Shepherd Is," stanza 1. We will then repeat the first verse by singing it in a two-part canon.

Hymn: "The King of Love My Shepherd Is" (ST. COLUMBA), stanza 1 (repeated in canon)

INVITATION TO PRAYER

Narrator: Prayer allows us to share with God what is on our minds and in our hearts. Sometimes we pray silently and at other times we pray aloud together. We know that God accepts us as we are and helps us to grow in faith through Jesus. Let us accept this invitation to pray by singing "It's Me, It's Me, O Lord."

Hymn: "It's Me, It's Me, O Lord" (PENITENT)

PRAYERS OF THE PEOPLE

Narrator: Jesus showed us that prayer enables us to reach God with our concerns, just like a ladder helps us to go beyond the limitations of our bodies. When we pray, we give thanks to God for all our blessings. We confess our wrongdoing and receive assurance of God's forgiveness. We pray for God's help in times of need, both for ourselves and others. Let us be in a mood of prayer, as we sing the first stanzas of "What a Friend We Have in Jesus" and "Sweet Hour of Prayer."

Hymns: "What a Friend We Have in Jesus" (CONVERSE), stanza 1
  "Sweet Hour of Prayer" (SWEET HOUR), stanza 1

Narrator: In one of our sessions, the children wrote individual prayers and tied them on our prayer ladder. They also wrote a group prayer, which they would like to share with you now.

Prayer from Session 3-A. *(The prayer is read by one or more of the children.)*

RESPONSE TO PRAYER

Narrator: We rejoice that a gracious God hears and answers our prayers. Let us respond by singing the refrain to stanza 1 of "Jesus Sang to Fishermen." The children will sing it through first and then we will all sing it together.

Hymn: "Jesus Sang to Fishermen" (BLACK MOUNTAIN), refrain for stanza 1

HEARING THE WORD

Narrator: In our community of faith, telling the "good news" of God's love for us in Jesus is central to our worship. Our first Bible reading is from Mark 10:13-16. In this short passage, Jesus is advocating, or speaking up, for the children. Listen to God's Word.

Scripture: Mark 10:13-16 *(read by a child)*

Narrator: Now let us sing two hymns that tell this story. Everyone will sing the familiar "Tell Me the Stories of Jesus," and then the children will stand and sing one stanza of a new hymn, "The People Came from Everywhere."

Hymns: "Tell Me the Stories of Jesus" (STORIES OF JESUS)
"The People Came from Everywhere" (CHILD'S PLAY)

Narrator: The second Bible reading is from Luke 18:9-14. Several of the children are going to dramatize this story, which Jesus told to teach people to be honest about who they are when they come to God in prayer. Watch and listen to God's Word.

Dramatized Scripture: "The Pharisee and the Tax Collector" (Luke 18:9-14)

THE SERMON

Narrator: After the Bible has been read, a pastor or someone from the congregation preaches a sermon to help us understand the message in that scripture. This is one way God still speaks to us today through Jesus. Instead of a spoken sermon, let us sing a hymn that proclaims the message we heard in the story of the Pharisee and the tax collector. The children will sing the first stanza of "Up to the Temple One Fine Day" by themselves, and then we will sing the rest of the hymn together.

Hymn: "Up to the Temple One Fine Day" (WHEATON), stanza 1: children; stanzas 2-5: all

RESPONDING TO THE WORD

Narrator: The offering is one of the ways we respond to God's word as a community of faith. Even in the earliest years of the church, believers brought bread and wine for the Lord's Supper and other food and gifts to share with the poor. In response to God's gracious generosity to us, let us now offer our gifts in return. Today's offering will be used for *[insert recipient(s)]*. As the offering is taken, let us sing stanzas 1, 2, and 4 of "There Is a Need for Shepherds," a hymn reminding us that God calls us to offer compassion, thoughtfulness, and time as well as money.

Hymn: "There Is a Need for Shepherds" (SHEPHERDS TODAY), stanzas 1, 2, and 4

GO IN GOD'S NAME

Narrator: As we leave this place to go out as God's people in a busy world, let us remember the blessings we have received in worship, and continue to find some quiet time to be with God each day. That is the message of our closing hymn, "Come Away with Me." Let us sing together stanzas 1 and 2.

Hymn: "Come Away with Me" (RECREATION), stanzas 1 and 2

BENEDICTION BY THE PASTOR

Narrator: The prayer at the end of a service of worship contains both a charge and a blessing. The pastor assures us of God's gracious love for us, and calls us to go in peace to love and serve our Lord Jesus Christ, with the help of the Holy Spirit.

Benediction *(Pastor)*

BENEDICTION RESPONSE

Narrator: After the spoken benediction, the congregation or choir may sing a response. Today the children will sing the refrain of the hymn, "Emmanuel, Who Walked Among Us Here."

Hymn: "Emmanuel, Who Walked Among Us Here" (KENSINGTON), refrain only

The King of Love My Shepherd Is

WORDS: Henry W. Baker
MUSIC: Irish melody; harm. from *The English Hymnal*, 1906

ST. COLUMBA

The King of Love My Shepherd Is

Orff Accompaniment

MUSIC: Irish melody; harm. from *The English Hymnal*, 1906

There Is a Need for Shepherds

WORDS: Mary Nelson Keithahn
MUSIC: John D. Horman
© 1992, 1997 Abingdon Press

SHEPHERDS TODAY

Refrain

door, _____ and home-less fam - ilies   long for home once
night, _____ and won - der why life   nev - er turns out
blame _____ on oth - ers for their   fail - ures and their
day _____ must shep-herd one an - oth - er in God's

more. _____
right. _____   There is a need for shep-herds in this
shame. _____
way. _____

hour. _____   There is a need for Love to show its power! _____

Tell Me the Stories of Jesus

WORDS: William H. Parker
MUSIC: Frederick A. Challinor

STORIES OF JESUS

The People Came from Everywhere

Unison

1. The peo - ple came from ev - 'ry - where to hear the Teach - er's
2. When Je - sus saw the chil - dren turn, their fac - es long and
3. "The ho - ly realm of God be - longs to chil - dren such as
4. As once you took your hands and blessed the chil - dren on their

news. _____ The _____ blind, the lame, the poor were there, en -
glum, _____ he _____ told his friends, "When will you learn that
these, _____ who _____ trust that God will right all wrongs, for -
way, _____ now _____ bless us, Je - sus, in our quest to

cour - aged by his views. _____ But those who brought the
lit - tle ones must come?" _____ He chi - ded them in -
give, and bring us peace. _____ If you would al - so
find your love, we pray. _____ We long to feel your

chil - dren near were quick - ly sent a - way: _____ "The _____
dig - nant - ly, "God's love can't be de - nied! _____ Let _____
now re - ceive the love that nev - er ends, _____ come _____
warm em - brace, and hear your kind - ly word, _____ that _____

WORDS: Mary Nelson Keithahn
MUSIC: John D. Horman
© 1997 Abingdon Press

CHILD'S PLAY

Teach - er's far too bus - y now. Don't both - er him to -
all the chil - dren come to me and sit here at my
as a trust - ing child, be - lieve in all that God in -
in the pres - ence of your grace our faith might be as -

day. _____ Don't both - er him to - day. _____
side, _____ come sit here at my side." _____
tends, _____ in all that God in - tends." _____
sured, _____ our faith that might be as - sured. _____

Sweet Hour of Prayer

1. Sweet hour of prayer! sweet hour of prayer! that calls me from _ a world of care,
2. Sweet hour of prayer! sweet hour of prayer! the joys I feel, _ the bliss I share
3. Sweet hour of prayer! sweet hour of prayer! thy wings shall my _ pe - ti - tion bear

and bids me at my Fa - ther's throne make all my wants _ and wish - es known.
of those whose anx - ious spir - its burn with strong de - sires _ for thy re - turn!
to him whose truth and faith - ful - ness en - gage the wait - ing soul to bless.

In sea - sons of dis - tress and grief, my soul has of - ten found re - lief,
With such I has - ten to the place where God my Sav - ior shows his face,
And since he bids me seek his face, be - lieve his word and trust his grace,

and oft es - caped the tempt - er's snare by thy re - turn, _ sweet hour of prayer!
and glad - ly take my sta - tion there, and wait for thee, _ sweet hour of prayer!
I'll cast on him my ev - ery care, and wait for thee, _ sweet hour of prayer!

WORDS: William Walford
MUSIC: William B. Bradbury

SWEET HOUR

Come Away with Me

1. Come a-way with me to a qui-et place, a-part from the world with its fran-tic pace, to pray, re-flect, and seek God's grace.
2. Come and pray with me on a gen-tle sea, on top of a hill in the Gal-i-lee, in gar-dens like Geth-se-ma-ne.
3. Come to-day with thoughts of the count-less ways that God's stead-fast love bless-es all our days, and join with me in si-lent praise.
4. Come and say, in words whis-pered from your soul, the feel-ings and ac-tions you can't con-trol. Your spir-it needs to be made whole.
5. Come a-way with me to a qui-et place, to God's lov-ing arms wait-ing to em-brace all those who come in hope of grace.

Refrain

Come a-way with me. Come a-way.

WORDS: Mary Nelson Keithahn
MUSIC: John D. Horman

RECREATION

Jesus Calls Us

1. Je - sus calls us o'er the tu - mult of our
2. As of old the a - pos - tles heard it by the
3. Je - sus calls us from the wor - ship of the
4. In our joys and in our sor - rows, days of
5. Je - sus calls us! By thy mer - cies, Sav - ior,

life's wild, rest - less sea; day by day his sweet voice
Gal - i - le - an lake, turned from home and toil and
vain world's gold - en store, from each i - dol that would
toil and hours of ease, still he calls, in cares and
may we hear thy call, give our hearts to thine o -

sound - eth, say - ing, "Chris - tian, fol - low me!"
kin - dred, leav - ing all for Je - sus' sake.
keep us, say - ing, "Chris - tian, love me more!"
plea - sures, "Chris - tian, love me more than these!"
be - dience, serve and love thee best of all.

WORDS: Cecil Frances Alexander
MUSIC: William H. Jude

GALILEE

Jesus Sang to Fishermen

WORDS: Mary Nelson Keithahn
MUSIC: John D. Horman
© 1997 Abingdon Press

BLACK MOUNTAIN

us, _____ sing to us, _____ sing to us, we pray. pray.

Come, Follow Me!
Movement Version

*Use with the accompaniment on page 82, continuing to echo-sing and move during the measures of rest.

WORDS and MUSIC: John D. Horman
© 2000 Abingdon Press

Come, Follow Me!
Echo Version

WORDS and MUSIC: John D. Horman
© 2000 Abingdon Press

Come, Follow Me!

Three-Part Canon Version

Come fol - low, fol - low, fol - low me!

Come fol - low me an - y - where that I lead.

Leave your boats, leave your nets! Come fol - low me!

WORDS and MUSIC: John D. Horman
© 2000 Abingdon Press

Come, Follow Me!

Four-Part Canon Version

Come fol - low, fol - low, fol - low me!

Come fol - low me an - y - where that I lead.

Leave your boats, leave your nets! Come fol - low me!

Trust in me and be - lieve! come fol - low me!

WORDS and MUSIC: John D. Horman
© 2000 Abingdon Press

Come, Follow Me!
Piano Accompaniment

MUSIC: John D. Horman
© 2000 Abingdon Press

Come, Follow Me!
Orff Accompaniment

MUSIC: John D. Horman
© 2000 Abingdon Press

What a Friend We Have in Jesus

1. What a friend we have in Je - sus, all our sins and griefs to bear!
2. Have we tri - als and temp - ta - tions? Is there trou - ble an - y - where?
3. Are we weak and heav - y la - den, cum - bered with a load of care?

What a priv - i - lege to car - ry ev - ery - thing to God in prayer!
We should nev - er be dis - cour - aged; take it to the Lord in prayer.
Pre - cious Sav - ior, still our ref - uge; take it to the Lord in prayer.

O what peace we of - ten for - feit, O what need - less pain we bear,
Can we find a friend so faith - ful who will all our sor - rows share?
Do thy friends de - spise, for - sake thee? Take it to the Lord in prayer!

all be - cause we do not car - ry ev - ery - thing to God in prayer.
Je - sus knows our ev - ery weak - ness; take it to the Lord in prayer.
In his arms he'll take and shield thee; thou wilt find a sol - ace there.

WORDS: Joseph M. Scriven
MUSIC: Charles C. Converse

CONVERSE

What a Friend We Have in Jesus

Rhythm Score

MUSIC: Charles C. Converse; arr. John D. Horman

Emmanuel, Who Walked Among Us Here

Unison

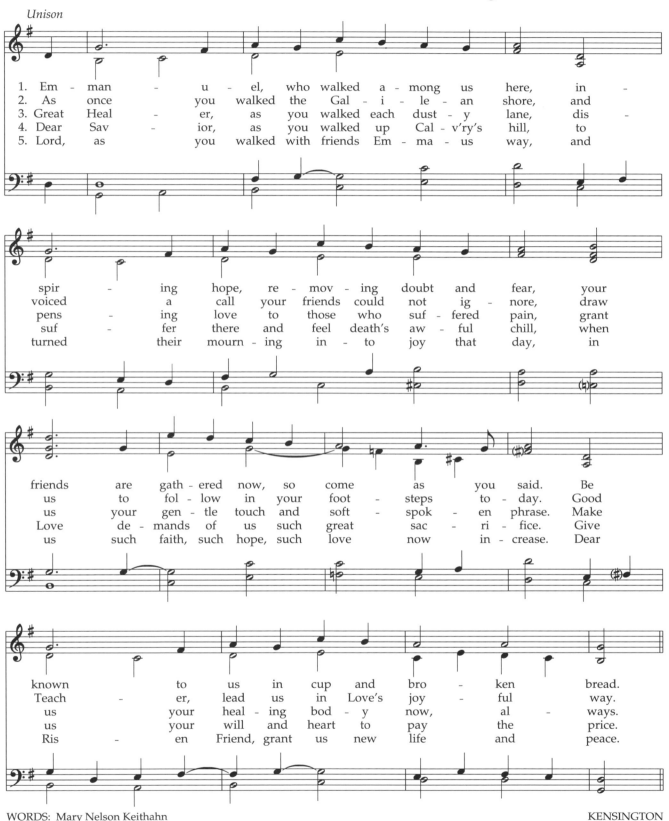

1. Em - man - u - el, who walked a - mong us here, in -
2. As once you walked the Gal - i - le - an shore, and
3. Great Heal - er, as you walked each dust - y lane, dis -
4. Dear Sav - ior, as you walked up Cal - v'ry's hill, to
5. Lord, as you walked with friends Em - ma - us way, and

spir - ing hope, re - mov - ing doubt and fear, your
voiced a call your friends could not ig - nore, draw
pens - ing love to those who suf - fered pain, grant
suf - fer there and those who feel death's aw - ful chill, grant
turned their mourn - ing in - to joy that day, in

friends are gath - ered now, so come as you said. Be
us to fol - low in your foot - steps to - day. Good
us your gen - tle touch and soft - spok - en phrase. Make
Love de - mands of us such great sac - ri - fice. Give
us such faith, such hope, such love now in - crease. Dear

known to us in cup and bro - ken bread.
Teach - er, lead us in Love's joy - ful way.
us your heal - ing bod - y now, al - ways.
us your will and heart to pay the price.
Ris - en Friend, grant us new life and peace.

WORDS: Mary Nelson Keithahn
MUSIC: John D. Horman
© 1997 Abingdon Press

KENSINGTON

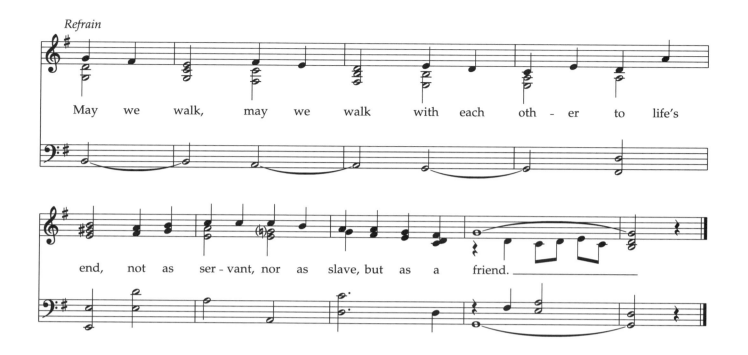

Refrain

May we walk, may we walk with each oth - er to life's end, not as ser - vant, nor as slave, but as a friend.

It's Me, It's Me, O Lord
(Standing in the Need of Prayer)

2. Not the preacher, not the deacon,
3. Not my father, not my mother,

WORDS: African American spiritual
MUSIC: African American spiritual; arr. by William Farley Smith

PENITENT

Up to the Temple One Fine Day

Unison

1. Up ___ to the Tem - ple one fine day went one who thought he
2. "How ___ glad I am to be u - nique! I'm strong where oth - er
3. Then, ___ stand - ing hum - bly far a - way, with no such righ - teous
4. Up ___ to the Tem - ple one fine day went two who thought they
5. God, ___ should we come to you in pride, re - mind us of our

knew ___ God's ___ way. This ___ Phar - i - see, so tall and proud,
men ___ are ___ weak. I ___ fast and tithe at your com - mand,
ré - su - mé, a ___ tax col - lec - tor bowed his head,
knew ___ God's ___ way, but ___ Je - sus said, in God's true sight,
sin - ful ___ side, that ___ all who wor - ship in this place

with arms up - raised, prayed ___ thus a - loud:
and walk with you, God, ___ hand in hand."
"For - give me, God, I've ___ sinned," he said.
the right was wrong, the ___ wrong was right.
might seek and find for - giv - ing grace.

WORDS: Mary Nelson Keithahn
MUSIC: John D. Horman
© 1996, 1997 Abingdon Press

WHEATON

God, you care for us like a shepherd.
You see that we are fed,
find us when we stray,
and keep us from all harm.
We are like sheep,
and sometimes lose our way,
but you sent Jesus, our Good Shepherd,
to bring us home to you.
For this, we sing our psalm of praise.
Be with us now, and all our days.
Amen.

I
am a
shepherd.
Do you
know
me?

Dear God, we are glad that Jesus told so many stories. We love to hear them, just as the children did so long ago. Thank you for helping Jesus be an advocate for them so they would not be turned away. We know Jesus is still speaking for children through all the people who care about us. Help us remember to thank them. Amen.

Come to the Hymn Sing

Presented by:

_____

_____

_____

Place:_____

Date:_____

Time:_____

Certificate of Participation

in

Something Old, SOMETHING NEW

Child's Name _____

Church _____

Teacher _____

Date _____

God loves me
for being me!

Index

Scripture References

Hymns

Hymn Writers/Composers of Something Old Sessions

Art and Bible Activities